Tribulation Worketh Patience
Living Triumphantly Through Faith and Enduring Hope

by

Floyd Bland

© 2022 by Floyd Bland, all rights reserved. No part of this book may be reproduced, transmitted, or stored except as provided under U.S. copyright laws.

This book is for Christian inspirational purposes and does not replace the advice or services of qualified clinical or legal professionals.

At press time, the author and publisher attempted to provide accurate subject matter. Neither the publisher nor author assumes any liability for loss or damage caused by content statements, errors, or omissions.

The author has altered persons or events for anonymity. Any similarity to actual persons, living or dead, entities, or locales is coincidental.

Unless otherwise noted, all Scripture quotations are from the New King James Version® (NKJV). Copyright © 1982 by Thomas Nelson. Used by permission. All rights reserved.

Scripture quotations marked (AKJV) are from the Authorized (King James) Version. Rights in the Authorized Version in the United Kingdom are vested in the Crown. Reproduced by permission of the Crown's patentee, Cambridge University Press

ISBN: 978-1-7325342-9-2
Library of Congress Control Number: 2022916823

And Hope Maketh Not Ashamed!

Contents

Many Thanks	vi
Introduction: What Happened to God's Divine Plan? *By Divine Appointment*	1
Chapter One: How Did We Get Here Anyway? *In the Beginning, A Systemic Plight: The Sin Problem, God Prepares Us for Intervention, God's Full Intervention*	10
Chapter Two: Tribulations and Trials *What We Aren't Exploring, Tribulations and Trials*	25
Chapter Three: But We Glory in Tribulations Also *Hemmed In, Our Divine Abnormality, We Glory in His Instruction and Direction*	44
Chapter Four: Tribulation Worketh Patience *Unseen Forces at Work, Abiding Under in Complete Surrender, Managing Our Emotions, Departing the Faith, Enduring Triumphantly*	60
Chapter Five: Patience Worketh Experience *Making the Grade, Partnering with God, Displaying God's Character, A Biblical Response*	80
Chapter Six: Experience Worketh Hope that Maketh not Ashamed *God is in Control, My Testimony, Final Thoughts*	109
About the Author	125

Many Thanks

As the years pass, I grow even more grateful to God for the love, grace, and mercy He extends to us through our Lord and Savior Jesus Christ.

To my beloved family, whose love, support, and encouragement have kept me committed to the task to "strengthen the brethren" and "bear fruit" for Christ, I thank you.

Thanks to Susan Robitaille of Second Look Editorial Services and Paramita Bhattacharjee of Creative Paramita Book Cover Designs for their expertise and professionalism in the preparation and design of this book for its publication.

Introduction

Introduction:
What Happened to God's Divine Plan?

By Divine Appointment

It is a memory blur now, but it happened after my graduation from elementary to junior high school (middle school today). It was an amazing time that I enjoyed with new friends—until one fateful day.

Scattered newspapers were everywhere, flying all over the sidewalk as my newspaper cart skidded down the hill and crashed into the front of the building a few feet behind me.

I was squatting on the pavement with both hands covering my face, stunned and emotionally deflated by the strategically-thrown punch that had just landed on my cheek. My combatant grumbled something at me I don't remember before returning up the hill.

I have wondered what would have happened if I had continued our impromptu skirmish. But in hindsight, discretion was the better part of valor by conceding defeat that day, because that crucial moment in my life was by Divine appointment.

Far more relieved than injured, I retrieved my cart, collected the strewn papers, and continued my deliveries, grateful that my harrowing experience was over—*and I survived!*

I seldom faced school conflict, because I hung around a group of unpretentious kids who were "non-existent" on the school's social radar. When not in class, I'd spend most of my time in the school library, which was my "window to the world" and haven from campus hostility.

There were those who hung out with the more popular "macho" crowd who often settled disagreements with fists (not guns, as is so prevalent in today's world).

I don't recall the details of the incident I witnessed that day, however, I do remember the principal calling me to his office to tell a small group of teachers, administrators, and an implicated classmate what misdeed I saw earlier that day.

The process was extremely unsettling for me, especially when my accused classmate gave me a look as I was leaving the room, which left no doubt that I was in some very *"deep yogurt!"*

The fear of grave danger tormented me the remainder of that school day, after it became clear that there would be a private student gathering after school, and I was the "guest of honor."

My classmate and I were from the same neighborhood, and we shared a unilateral "code for snitches," for people who reported others' actions to the authorities. Thus, I expected to be "taught a lesson" for my infraction. I didn't know how or when, but I reckoned that something painful was in my immediate future.

I suppose I could have asked a friend to "watch out" for me while I delivered the newspapers that afternoon, but I didn't. I figured it was my problem, and that somehow it would work out. I was alone, but not really. God was there to accompany me.

I took special precautions to service my last customers first and my first ones last to avoid passing common areas. However, my clever scheme backfired as my "street-smart" disputant cornered me near the hilltop center point of my paper route.

This was a faith-defining moment for me, an impressionable teenager whose heart still resonated with excitement about the vast possibilities God had given me at my church's school and college recognition ceremony recently.

As I stood before the church with the other graduates, I knew that God's favor was in my life. Especially after the pastor's wife presented me with a new Bible and recited this unforgettable Scripture passage during the ceremony,

> Trust in the LORD with all thine heart; and lean not unto thine own understanding. In all thy ways acknowledge him, and he shall direct thy paths. Proverbs 3:5-6 (AKJV)

Years before, I had placed my faith in Jesus Christ as my personal Lord and Savior and had become very active in my church, where they recognized me as one of their future Christian leaders.

Mom, Dad, and Grandma, along with countless other mature Christians, mostly affiliated with our church, taught me how to read (and study) my Bible and share my faith.

The Lord blessed me with solid Christian mentors who showed me how to fast, pray, memorize Bible verses, and perform other ascetic disciplines to enhance my spiritual and moral development.

Under their discipleship and guidance, I learned how to practice my Christian faith by serving my church as a Junior Layman, then as a Junior Deacon, and later as the Bible Reader Leader for our Baptist Training Union.

I sang in the Youth Choir, joined our church's evangelistic team to serve at a local rescue mission/soup kitchen, and I took part in other community outreach church initiatives to help people in need whenever and whenever I could.

As a result, I anticipated the Lord would fulfill this very special promise (_my emphasis_),

> When a man's ways please the LORD, _He makes even his enemies to be at peace with him_. (Proverbs 16:7)

Because I lived a "Christian life," I believed the Lord's goodness and mercy would follow me all the days of my life.

I was convinced that no weapon formed against me would prosper, because if God was for me, as Psalm 23:6, Isaiah 54:17, and Romans 8:31 declare, then who could be against me?

I also trusted in the captivating, metaphorical images in Scripture where the Psalmist describes God's constant vigilance to guarantee our safety,

> He who dwells in the secret place of the Most High Shall abide under the shadow of the Almighty. I will say of the LORD, "He is my refuge and my fortress; My God, in Him I will trust." Surely He shall deliver you from the snare of the fowler And from the perilous pestilence. He shall cover you with His feathers, And under His wings you shall take refuge; His truth shall be your shield and buckler. You shall not be afraid of the terror by night, Nor of the arrow that flies by day, Nor of the pestilence that walks in darkness, Nor of

the destruction that lays waste at noonday. A thousand may fall at your side, And ten thousand at your right hand; But it shall not come near you. (Psalm 91:1-7)

Moreover, my Almighty Protector keeps me secure in His hands, and I am "bound in the bundle of the living with the Lord" my God. (*cf.*, 1 Samuel 25:29, John 10:28-29)

Yet, this one paradoxical moment triggered my engagement in a classic theological debate I will summarize here,

> God is our Beneficent Creator and Sovereign Ruler. Among His many noble attributes are holiness, truth, justice, faithfulness, and love. His goodness motivates Him to satisfy our deepest longings for everything we could ever wish for, desire, or imagine. By His mercy, we can know and enjoy His all-encompassing plan for our reclamation, redemption, and reconciliation. *Then, why does God allow His precious Children to suffer pain and misfortune?*

I may not have asked that question or its counterpart, *"Why do bad things happen to good people?"* that day. Yet, I have asked both questions many times since.

Not long after my epiphany, while reading the Authorized King James Version of the Bible, the Lord led me to a Scripture passage that helped me to understand how He uses trials to refine our spiritual, physical, and emotional dispositions,

> But we glory in tribulations also: knowing that tribulation worketh patience; And patience, experience; and experience, hope: And hope maketh not ashamed; because the love of God is shed abroad in our hearts by the Holy Ghost which is given unto us. Romans 5:3-5 (AKJV)

For two-thousand years, these enduring truths have encouraged and strengthened God's people during difficult times. Over the next few pages, we will explore them using this outline,

Chapter One: How Did We Get Here Anyway?
Chapter Two: Our Tribulations and Trials
Chapter Three: We Glory in Tribulations Also
Chapter Four: Tribulation Worketh Patience
Chapter Five: Patience Worketh Experience
Chapter Six: Experience Worketh Hope that
            Maketh not Ashamed

Although archaic, I will use some King James' phrasing to maintain consistency. I have also inserted capitalized nouns and pronouns that relate to the Lord and His Kingdom to preserve doctrinal content and theological clarity as well.

As we look at how we got here in the next chapter, I pray the Lord uses these testimonies to perfect, establish, strengthen, and settle your faith and your love for Him. (1 Peter 5:10)

Chapter One

Chapter One:
How Did We Get Here Anyway?

In the Beginning
To understand our tribulation better, we should start at the beginning, when God created a perfect world where we could share in His eternal bliss.

Before we sinned, or the Fall, we had intimacy with God as our constant Friend and Companion. We felt His love in full measure, which gave us unending joy and satisfaction. As our Faithful Provider, God gave us all we needed to live in full contentment.

To water the plants and trees that gave us esthetically pleasing, delicious, and nutritious fruits and vegetables, He designed a perfect subterranean irrigation system.

Clothing was unnecessary in our climate-controlled environment with neither rain nor storms. In our perfect setting, God protected, nurtured, and provided for us thoroughly.

God created the human species "in His image," elevated and distinct from all other earthly creatures.

He made us perfectly, as male and female, to procreate, to be good stewards over the earth, and to exercise dominion over the animal kingdom. (Genesis 1:27-28) One author relates it this way,

> In making man after his own image, therefore, God endowed him with those attributes which belong to his own nature as a spirit. Man is thereby distinguished from all other inhabitants of this world, and raised immeasurably above them. He belongs to the same order of being as God Himself, and is therefore capable of communion with his Maker. This conformity of nature between man and God, is not only the distinguishing prerogative of humanity, so far as earthly creatures are concerned, but it is also the necessary condition of our capacity to know God, and therefore the foundation of our religious nature. If we were not like God, we could not know Him.[1]

In that idyllic setting—free from sin, pain, sorrow, illness, fear, or death—we experienced His holiness, peace, and joy in full measure. In every way, we prospered and flourished abundantly.

There was one caveat. We could not eat from the Tree of the Knowledge of Good and Evil. (Genesis 2:16–17) Subsequently, we disobeyed God and fell from our perfection.

A Systemic Plight: The Sin Problem

Here is how one author describes the Fall of humanity with its tragic outcomes,

> [The Fall is] the original act of Adam and Eve when they disobeyed God and lost their intimate relationship with him (Genesis 3). They fell from perfect communion with God to a state of imperfect communion with him. By this act sin entered into the life of the human race in that instead of enjoying the fact of being God's creatures, human beings lacked a meaningful and loving relationship with their Creator.[2]

Once our ancestors ate the forbidden fruit, they lost their perfection, exchanging it for sin, decay, and death.

The most devastating outcome was universal sin, which resulted in our immediate separation from God—for all have sinned. (Romans 3:23)

Here is a short comparison of our pre- and post-Fall conditions,

Before the Fall	After the Fall
Total perfection and complete fulfillment.	Imperfection, guilt, shame, and unfulfillment.
A daily companionship with God as Friend.	Eternal separation from God as enemies and adversaries.
Beautiful and bountiful provisions in Eden.	A world of thorns, blight, illness, pain, and death.
Recipients of God's joy, and pleasure forever.	Toil, struggle, and suffering in everything we do.
Peace and tranquility abound everywhere.	Anxiety and uncertainty in every phase of life.

Yearning to know and love God personally.	An aversion toward God and godly things.
A union with God; free from sin and death.	Sin and death subjugates and taints us thoroughly.

Separated from our Loving Creator, we have a "God sized" spiritual vacuum inside us that yearns to restore our pre-Fall intimacy with the Lord.

Some will look to family to fill the void but will not find it there. For more often than not, our family members are broken and empty, seeking solutions to fill the void for themselves.

We turn to our friends and society for relief, but find that, as sin grows more rampant in our world each day, cold indifference is often the outcome, just as Jesus foretold in Matthew 24:12.

We then turn to our professions with careers in science and medicine, business and enterprise, information technology, finance, sales and marketing, education and academia, law and politics, or sports, travel and entertainment to gain wealth, power, and influence hoping to fill the void.

But we discover that even after achieving those magnificent accomplishments, the void remains, and we feel empty, alone, and frustrated and realize we live in a cold, cruel, and unfulfilling world.

To escape our inner emptiness, we try splurging on the newest, biggest, and shiniest thing we can afford, convinced that it will bring us internal satisfaction and instant gratification.

But inanimate objects will not comfort us like the wonderful blessing of God's tender, loving companionship, and we feel more empty and unfulfilled.

When that does not work, we turn to sensual pleasures (i.e., gluttony, sex, pornography, marital infidelity, drugs, alcohol, other intoxicants, etc.) to find euphoria. However, we learn that our self-medicating, self-numbing, and self-gratifying will not quell our inner turmoil and spiritual suffering.

We soon learn that a compulsive-addictive lifestyle will not give us the metaphysical relief we seek. Instead, it fosters counter-productive thoughts, speech, and conduct that promote our own self-destruction while contravening the overall safety and well-being for others as well.

Our failures cause intense feelings of anxiety, self-pity, anger, frustration, and depression. Unable to return to God because of our sin, and opposed to His Law because of our sin nature, we try to fill our spiritual void "our way,"

> For I bear them witness that they have a zeal for God, but not according to knowledge. For they being ignorant of

God's righteousness, and seeking to establish their own righteousness, have not submitted to the righteousness of God. (Romans 10:2-3)

As Adam and Eve's sin-tainted offspring, we tend to reject following the ordinances of God, just as they did.

We also rely on subterfuge to avoid personal accountability with impunity. Sin's insidiousness causes us to behave poorly, even when we have noble intentions,

> The heart is deceitful above all things, and desperately wicked: who can know it? Jeremiah 17:9 (AKJV)

Our human depravity prevents us from achieving moral and spiritual perfection, as this author notes,

> [Original Sin is] a term to denote the effect of Adam's sin upon the moral life of his descendants. It is formally defined as "that whereby man is very far gone from original righteousness, and is of his own nature inclined to evil"... The fact of sin in this sense is plainly proclaimed in Scripture ... and borne witness to by history and human self-consciousness.[3]

Some will argue that we are not inherently hateful, self-serving, or prejudice, and that we can perform good deeds without malice.

Although we can perform good deeds, our sin-tainted nature skews our moral compass to produce immoral outcomes—consistently.

> There is a way that seems right to a man,
> But its end is the way of death. (Proverbs 14:12)

We all sin, and as the Bible teaches, "If we say that we have no sin, we deceive ourselves, and the truth is not in us." (1 John 1:8)

In addition, "good people" suffer from sin's collateral damage (e.g., pain, fear, guilt, shame, depression, cognitive failure, doubt, and death).

It is as if Adam and Eve's disobedience tilted our world forty-five degrees, and we have been sliding down its slippery slope since.

Human kindness, technology, wealth, influence, and notoriety can be a productive means to an end, but they will not alter our downward trajectory.

We can never escape God's reckoning. Sin's price is death, which means eternal separation from God, because He is holy, and His response to sin is judgment (wrath).

Thus, we are "children of wrath," who are sliding toward a fiery Hell where the worms never die, and the fire burns forever. (*cf.*, Ephesians 2:3, Mark 9:48)

God Prepares Us for Intervention
Sin restricts our access to God, since only "perfect" people occupy His "perfect" world. Yet, it remains God's desire for us to live with Him uncontaminated by sin.

To do so, He will create a new Heaven and new earth where His righteousness prevails. There, He will reestablish His perfect environment where we can know His loving fellowship, beauty, bounty, and perfection forever, where the wicked will cease from troubling, and the weary will rest. For this fulfillment, His entire creation eagerly awaits. (*cf.* Job 3:17, Isaiah 65:17, Romans 8:19-23, 2 Peter 3:10-13, Revelation 21:1-4)

In the meantime, He gave us short-term ways to remediate sin by instituting blood as the means to achieve Atonement. (*cf.*, Leviticus 17:11, Hebrews 9:22) Here is how one author describes our necessity for God's wonderful atoning work,

> The Bible teaches that there is something in the nature of God to which sin is so offensive, so infinitely hateful, as to excite his holy wrath. It may be said, too, that sin is the only thing in the universe that has

ever excited the wrath of God. That moral quality of the divine nature which causes hatred of sin excites wrath against sin, and therefore makes necessary an atonement, in order that sin may be pardoned.[4]

Animal blood was a short-term fix to pardon sin, make us righteous, and restore our broken fellowship. However, only someone without sin, with pristine blood, could satisfy God's righteousness and remediate our sin.

God's Full Intervention

Our sin-tainted blood was inadequate, so God Himself intervened by becoming the Perfect Man in Jesus Christ and paid sin's price—completely. (*cf.*, Isaiah 53:4-6, Hebrews 9:11-15)

By faith in Him, He bestows us eternal life so that we can experience His perfect plan—our eternal salvation (*my emphasis*),

> For God so loved the world that He gave His only begotten Son, *that whoever believes in Him should not perish but have everlasting life.* For God did not send His Son into the world to condemn the world, but that the world through Him might be saved. (John 3:16–17)

When we turn to Jesus Christ, as our personal Lord and Savior, we become Born Again. At that precise moment, His Holy Spirit fills that "God-size void" to enliven (quicken) us spiritually.

Instantly, we come to know His selfless love and experience His lasting peace, joy, fulfillment, and deep satisfaction as He transforms us into His new creations,

> Therefore, if anyone is in Christ, he is a new creation; old things have passed away; behold, all things have become new. (2 Corinthians 5:17)

It is just as if God's Spirit turns on a "no longer dead but alive" switch inside us; for the first time, we understand what "real" living is all about.

Another benefit is how God gives us Jesus' righteousness. Just as our sin-tainted blood will not cover sin, our sin-tainted "good" works will not make us righteous. Yet, faith in Christ will, most emphatically,

> Therefore, having been justified by faith, we have peace with God through our Lord Jesus Christ, through whom also we have access by faith into this grace in which we stand, and rejoice in hope of the glory of God. (Romans 5:1-2)

Justified means that when God looks at us, He no longer sees our sin. (We are now in Christ.) He sees Jesus' righteousness instead.

Eternal redemption and reconciliation comes with our new standing in Christ, or Justification, by which God expunges our sin record, as this author observes,

> Justification is a judicial or forensic act, i.e., an act of God as judge proceeding according to law, declaring that the sinner is just, i.e., that the law no longer condemns him, but acquits and pronounces him to be entitled to eternal life.[5]

In addition, eternal peace of mind is ours as feelings of calm, ease, assurance, and satisfaction replace our worries, anxieties, doubts, and fears. Now we know God has accepted us into His family, and we can constantly reflect on His goodness and mercy,

> You will keep him in perfect peace, Whose mind is stayed on You, Because he trusts in You. (Isaiah 26:3)

We enjoy eternal peace and favor with God, along with all the blessings we will ever need in this life and the next. Herein lies our source of great comfort,

> Blessed are those who mourn, For they shall be comforted. (Matthew 5:4)

Even with the Holy Spirit abiding within us, we will never reach perfection in this life; we will sin occasionally. However, instead of trying to hide our sin by making excuses for them, we confess them and ask the Lord and the offended person(s) for forgiveness.

We also grow to forgive ourselves by "closing the book" on our past and resolve not to repeat the same offense. This is another wonderful benefit we have in Christ,

> Brethren, I do not count myself to have apprehended; but one thing I do, forgetting those things which are behind and reaching forward to those things which are ahead, I press toward the goal for the prize of the upward call of God in Christ Jesus. Philippians 3:13-14

We are mindful that the blood of Jesus covers our sins, and since God has forgiven us, we can forgive others and ourselves equally.

Our spiritual transformation is unlike anything we could have ever known or experienced in this life before coming to Christ. The Lord makes this distinction in His wonderful promise of John 10:10,

> The thief does not come except to steal, and to kill, and to destroy. I have come

that they may have life, and that they may have it more abundantly.

Our lives grow more abundantly each day as His Spirit and His Word (Bible) reveal how we can know and love Him as our Blessed Redeemer and Merciful Savior.

We become His offspring, and like newborn babes, we yearn for more of His presence and a greater level of intimacy with Him. Christ in us is our ever-increasing hope of glory. (Colossians 1:27)

Our "good" works, which were "filthy rags" before coming to Christ, now follow us as we express our gratitude for God's grace and mercy extended toward us. (*cf.*, Isaiah 64:6, Ephesians 2:10)

Despite God's glorious intervention, sin and death still prevail on earth to affect us all. Thus, tribulations and trials are phenomena we will endure—for life!

In this chapter, we looked at how we got here. In the next, we will explore tribulations and trials.

Notes

[1] Charles Hodge, "Man Created in the Image of God," *Systematic Theology*, vol. II, 3rd printing, (Peabody: Hendrickson Publishers, 2003) 97.

[2] J.D. Douglas, Walter A. Ewell, and Peter Toon, "Fall, The," *The Concise Dictionary of the Christian Tradition: Doctrine, Liturgy, History*, (Grand Rapids: Regency Reference Library, 1989) 150, also see: William L. Reese, "Sin," *Dictionary of Philosophy and Religion: Eastern and Western Thought*, 8th ed., (Atlantic Highlands, NJ: Humanities Press, 1980) 530, and Cecil B. Murphey, "Sin and Virtue," *The Dictionary of Biblical Literacy*, (Nashville: Thomas Nelson, 1989) 460-466.

[3] See: Merrill F. Unger, "Original Sin," *Unger's Bible Dictionary*, 3rd ed., 18th printing, (Chicago: Moody, 1972) 1028.

[4] James Madison Pendleton, "The Necessity of the Atonement," *Christian Doctrines: A Compendium of Theology*, 33rd printing, (Valley Forge: Judson Press, 1976) 234.

[5] Charles Hodge, "Justification," *Systematic Theology*, vol. III, 3rd printing, (Peabody: Hendrickson Publishers, 2003) 119.

Chapter Two

Chapter Two:
Tribulations and Trials

What We Aren't Exploring

As human beings, we share the universal plight of tribulation and trial from the external pressures in our normal, day-to-day lives. Before examining tribulation, however, let's clarify what it's not.

Not the Great Tribulation
We will not explore the turbulent period forecasted in Daniel 12, Matthew 24, and throughout Revelation, when Christians suffer worldwide persecution for their faith in Jesus Christ.

Persecution for the Christian faith remains a horrible reality for many today, as it did the First Century Church, as one writer explains,

> Therefore, a merely external suffering, such as anybody may have, is not meant thereby, but the cross as a consequence of Christian faith. Faith leads into tribulation, because as peace with God, it leads into conflict with the kingdom of darkness, and also with sin in ourselves, because it endows the ordinary suffering of this life with a spiritual character.[1]

Another writer puts it this way,

> Christians are not exempt from tribulation, but rather they are especially subject to it. Their tribulation consists largely of persecution and the opposition their testimony meets in an unfriendly world. ... Tribulation, then, to the early Christians meant not so much ill health, poverty or loss of friends, but the sacrifices they had to make and the perils they had to meet from their proclamation or profession of Christ. ... Tribulation is the appointed destiny of Christians.[2]

We live in the "Last Days," when our Enemy, (Satan, or the Devil), is deluding many people into elevating the material and temporal above the transcendent and eternal.

We will not live in this world forever, and beyond this life, there is a vast eternity before us. Psalm 90:10 gives seventy to eighty years as our earthly lifespan, some living more or fewer.

Yet far too many of us place a greater emphasis on the "here and now" with a mindset that says, "*He who lives three-score and ten with the most toys wins!*" Nevertheless, I have yet to see a moving van containing the deceased's personal effects following the funeral procession.

We will not leave this earth alive. Neither will we take any personal possessions with us when it's our time to die. Thus, it would be prudent to make plans for the soul to avoid eternal peril,

> For what is a man profited, if he shall gain the whole world, and lose his own soul? or what shall a man give in exchange for his soul? (Matthew 16:26)

Also in these Last Days, the Enemy has deceived us into thinking that it is ok to ignore or disregard God's Word and our God-given human dignity by mocking biblical principles and reducing human worth to something that we can buy or sell cheap.

We see this in the indiscriminate killing of the unborn and helpless, euthanizing the weak and aged, and the exploitation, abuse, and violence directed toward innocent victims.

The Devil is a formidable Enemy, just as the Scriptures warn,

> Be sober, be vigilant; because your adversary the devil walks about like a roaring lion, seeking whom he may devour. (1 Peter 5:8)

Ours is not a perfect world. Yet, there was a time when applying universal biblical principles that distinguish right from wrong dominated our social context. We respected and welcomed prayer, the Ten Commandments, and other Judeo-Christian values.

We distinguished proper from improper conduct to sustain social stability, maintain civil order, and protect our most vulnerable citizens. Yet, today, we vilify the righteous and reward the wicked.

We may not be in the Great Tribulation, but "modern society" encourages its citizens to worship the state, power, money, and the occult instead of God. It also is working feverishly to sanitize society of all Judeo-Christian values under the pretense of "separation of church and state."

In these Last Days, the antithesis of our free society, which allows us to espouse and practice biblical values, is the repressive communist society that portrays itself as "god" as this writer observes,

> Yes, the Communist Party became a god. The mind of man has been so created by God so that it cannot function as an autonomous entity. It must have ultimate truth, a final authority, a god it sees as the fountainhead of all values and from which all final truth is derived. Having denied the existence of the living and true God, Marxism in cynical contradiction turned to atheism to create a god for man to serve joyfully—the Party.[3]

Some of these ideals are creeping into the very fabric of our culture where we worship a failed, godless Marxist-Leninist ideology that people endorse around the world, as the author continues,

> At the core of its philosophy and conduct is the conviction and the oft-repeated announcement, "There is no God." The absence of God is not simply another acceptable philosophic point of view, among many others. Rather, it is the denial of the Christian claim—yes, the teachings of the Bible—that there is a just, holy, loving, and personal God who has created the universe and who presides over its continuance.[4]

Godless ideologies influence our politics, business, schools, colleges, media, and clergy to advocate an empty utopian promise that we can provide for ourselves—apart from the true God.

Censoring all biblically-centered principles that refute the godless "everything is relative" and "everyone is right" ideologies is essential.

Consequently, the philosophy that humanity has no need for God, Jesus Christ, or the Bible fills the moral vacuum. All by ourselves, we can achieve prosperity, fulfillment, and peace—*for the elite only.*

Yet, all our attempts to purge God from our consciousness have been to our detriment; not benefit, just as the Bible warns,

> Woe unto them that call evil good, and good evil; that put darkness for light, and light for darkness; that put bitter for sweet, and sweet for bitter. Isaiah 5:20 (AKJV)

Political and social anarchy follows any society that rejects God. This author relates the domestic upheaval that contributed to a nation's downfall,

> I have reserved for the last the most potent and forcible cause of destruction, the domestic hostilities of the Romans themselves. ... In a dark period of five hundred years Rome was perpetually afflicted by the sanguinary quarrels of the nobles and the people . . . At such a time, when every quarrel was decided by the sword, and none could trust their lives or properties to the impotence of law, the powerful citizens were armed for safety, or offense, against the domestic enemies whom they feared or hated.[5]

Throughout history, countries have sought to eradicate God from its civic, social, and moral ethos and failed.

Can't we learn from history that technology, education, politics, military, sports, or industry do not make a nation great?

The hallmark of any great nation is its cherished faith in God expressed in proper moral and spiritual standards, just as the Scriptures attest,

> Righteousness exalts a nation, but sin is a reproach to any people. (Proverbs 14:34)

Also,

> When it goes well with the righteous, the city rejoices; And when the wicked perish, there is jubilation. By the blessing of the upright the city is exalted, But it is overthrown by the mouth of the wicked. (Proverbs 11:10-11)

Zechariah 4:6 tells us we cannot achieve greatness through our own prowess. It is God's spiritual presence and power working through us that allows us to achieve greatness and prosperity.

Doomed to utter ruin is the nation that turns its back on God and His righteous living principles while preying on its vulnerable citizens.

Not Self-Inflicted Consequences
I will not link tribulations with the collateral damage from our poor choices, reckless living, and/or contemptible conduct.

Job 14:1 tells us our time on earth is full of trouble. Thus, I concede that our human selfishness, sinful nature, and Satan can influence us to exercise our free will in ways that muddle God's very best outcomes for us in every phase of our lives.

We reap what we sow. (Galatians 6:7-8) Sowing immorality reaps pain and suffering, and the blatant defiance of God's laws through irresponsible and reckless behavior or "sowing the wind," results in our "reaping the whirlwind." (Hosea 8:7)

No one individual lives, functions, or dies within society without affecting all citizens. Together, we are joint stakeholders who matter to each other as "our brother's keeper." (Genesis 4:9)

In a civil society, our social freedoms come with the responsibility of constraint, since we can easily use them to exploit and/or victimize others. Our freedom of expression should never endanger another person's health or safety.

Ours is a shared sacred trust to preserve public civility, decency, and goodwill and to avoid the possibility of being unfortunate victims when another person's free expression harms us.

We should never do what we want, when we want, to whomever we want willy-nilly without first performing the noble acts of courtesy, civility, and understanding. It is up to civilized people to preserve the free exercise of our moral responsibility by extending fundamental consideration toward our fellow citizens,

> The freedom of God is exercised and illustrated in his government of his moral creatures. It has pleased God to create intelligences possessed of moral freedom and to make their ultimate destiny contingent upon the right use of their freedom.[6]

Thank God for the civic and moral laws we have in place to guard against pursuing our personal freedom at the expense of another person's pursuit of life, liberty, and happiness.

We share the world with other people, so it would behoove us to foster an atmosphere of goodwill. Such is in all of our best interests, since no rational person wants to live where there is constant anarchy, hostility, and violence.

Tribulations and Trials
Everyone experiences tribulations and trials since they are the unfortunate byproducts of a fallen, sin-broken world.

The non-believer has no recourse but to endure them—but without God. Often, they become frustrated and angry with the Lord and blame Him for their misfortune, as the Word tells us,

> The foolishness of a man twists his way,
> And his heart frets against the Lord.
> (Proverbs 19:3)

God reassures the believer that He is with us to see us through our adversities. Just as His Word declares, we will not face these challenges alone,

> Yea, though I walk through the valley of the shadow of death, I will fear no evil; For You are with me. (Psalm 23:4)

> When you pass through the waters, I will be with you; And through the rivers, they shall not overflow you. When you walk through the fire, you shall not be burned, Nor shall the flame scorch you. For I am the Lord your God, The Holy One of Israel, your Savior (Isaiah 43:2-3a)

> I am with you always, even to the end of the age. (Matthew 28:20)

For the Christian, tribulations and trials are synonymous terms that describe the events or circumstances that cause us pain, distress, or suffering.

Tribulations perform far more good within us than they pose harm to us. God uses them to affect our spiritual growth as His righteous Children, who are suitable for eternal fellowship.

> The refining pot is for silver and the furnace for gold, But the LORD tests the hearts. (Proverbs 17:3)

Sometimes, God uses them to accomplish His will for a specified period. He might also use them to develop essential qualities within us—primarily faith and integrity—that make us more like Christ.

The Holy Spirit, who abides within us, gives us the strength to endure our adversities while He brings about His positive outcomes, blessings, and fulfillment.

We will find God's abiding presence, favor, and comfort to confront our circumstances with His joy, which is our strength as well (Nehemiah 8:10), as the Psalmist observes also,

> The Lord is my strength and my shield; My heart trusted in Him, and I am helped; Therefore my heart greatly rejoices, And with my song I will praise Him. The Lord is their strength, And He is the saving refuge of His anointed. (Psalm 28:7-8)

Tribulations also make us more dependent upon the Lord to fight our battles and to supply our every need.

Each tribulation that God resolves for us fosters our confidence and trust as He shows Himself as faithful and reliable in every situation,

> I will lift up my eyes to the hills—From whence comes my help? My help comes from the Lord, Who made heaven and earth. (Psalm 121:1-2)

God is the giver of every "good and perfect" gift. He will not use tribulation to cause harm or lead us to sin. Satan and/or our sin nature will induce unhealthy, lustful desires in us that often lead to poor choices and wicked behavior. (James 1:14)

Instead, the Lord helps us to grow spiritually so that we can overcome temptation progressively. He strengthens our moral character, just as He promises,

> No temptation has overtaken you except such as is common to man; but God is faithful, who will not allow you to be tempted beyond what you are able, but with the temptation will also make the way of escape, that you may be able to bear it. (1 Corinthians 10:13)

God uses tribulation to lead us in the path of righteousness so that He gets the credit for performing what is always in our best interests. (*cf.*, Psalm 23:3, James 1:17)

Old Testament Tribulation
The Old Testament Hebrew *"sar,"* (Strong OT 6862),[7] translated as tribulation, establishes the idea of one being in a narrow space (or hemmed in) to illustrate pain, distress, or oppression.

Moses uses this word in his final address to the Children of Israel in Deuteronomy 4:30-31. There, he tells how God will use tribulation to help His wayward people consider returning to Him for restoration and relief,

> When you are in [tribulation], and all these things come upon you in the latter days, when you turn to the Lord your God and obey His voice (for the Lord your God is a merciful God), He will not forsake you nor destroy you, nor forget the covenant of your fathers which He swore to them.

Old Testament Trial
There are Old Testament passages that use variants of the word trial, Hebrew *"sarap,"* (Strong OT 6884/TWOT 1972),[8] which presents the idea of smelting and refining.

The imagery is much like the goldsmith or silversmith who refines precious metals with heat. God tries, proves, refines, or examines our hearts/minds through trial,

> For thou, O God, hast proved us: thou hast [refined] us, as silver is [refined]. (Psalm 66:10)

In addition, the Hebrew "*bahan*," (Strong OT 974/TWOT 230),[9] also translated as trial, expresses how God uses trial to examine us for essential human characteristics (i.e., faith, integrity, etc.), as this Scripture passage relates,

> I, the Lord, search the heart, I [try/test] the mind, Even to give every man according to his ways, According to the fruit of his doings. (Jeremiah 17:10)

New Testament Tribulation
In the New Testament, we translate the Greek word "*thlipsis*," (Strong NT 2347),[10] as tribulation, to express a crushing, pressing, compressing, or squeezing. The word implies a connection between external circumstances and human tribulation, as Romans 5:3 implies,

> And not only that, but we also glory in [tribulations], knowing that [tribulation] produces perseverance.

New Testament Trial
The New Testament Greek "*dokimion*," (Strong NT1383),[11] translated as trial, describes the idea of testing, proof, or trustworthiness to convey being tested through affliction to show something (e.g.,

us, our faith, or God) has proven to be reliable and authentic, as 1 Peter 1:6-7 express,

> In this you greatly rejoice, though now for a little while, if need be, you have been grieved by various trials, that the [trial] of your faith, being much more precious than gold that perishes, though it is tested by fire, may be found to praise, honor, and glory at the revelation of Jesus Christ.

Greek derivatives *"dokime,"* (Strong NT1382), *"dokimos,"* (Strong NT1384), and *"dokimazo,"* (Strong NT1381),[12] show how something tried has passed the test.

They can also tell how something is concrete, authentic, and verified after having been proven or tested, as presented here,

> For to this end I also wrote, that I might put you to the [trial/test], whether you are obedient in all things. (2 Corinthians 2:9)

> Blessed is the man who endures temptation; for when he has been [tried/tested], he will receive the crown of life which the Lord has promised to those who love Him. Let no one say when he is tempted, "I am tempted by God"; for God cannot be tempted by evil, nor does He Himself tempt anyone. (James 1:12-13)

> But as we have been [tried/approved] by God to be entrusted with the gospel, even so we speak, not as pleasing men, but God who [tries/examines] our hearts. (1 Thessalonians 2:4)

When we respond nobly in adversity, the Lord deems us as approved.

As the sun that shines and the rain that falls on the just and the unjust alike (Matthew 5:45), highs and lows; abundance and adversity; fulfillment and frustration; tribulation and trial are all common life cycles we can expect during our pilgrimage on earth—even though God is with us.

Here is how one author summarizes our Christian journey as we encounter tribulation and trial,

> The believer glories in tribulations because he knows they will bring clearer vision of what lies ahead—hope with conviction in it. The order of these verses is significant—tribulation, endurance, character, and then hope. Testing brings the response of endurance. Endurance produces character. The outcome of all this is hope. Hope does not disappoint.[13]

In this chapter, we looked at tribulations and trials that affect us all. In the next chapter, we will look at how we can glory in our tribulations also.

Notes

[1] J.P. Lange, "Epistle of Paul to the Romans," *Commentary on the Holy Scriptures: Critical, Doctrinal and Homiletical*, Philip Schaff, trans., 7th ed., vol. 10, (Grand Rapids: Zondervan, 1980) 168.

[2] Spiros Zodhiates, "θλίψις," *The Complete Word Study Dictionary, New Testament*, rev. ed., (Chattanooga: AMG International, 1993) 737.

[3] Dave Breese, "The Ruling Principle for all Humanity: Karl Marx," *Seven Men Who Rule the World from the Grave*, (Chicago: Moody Press, 1990) 71.

[4] For further discussion, see: Dave Breese, *op. cit.*, 67, and William L. Reese, "Marxism," *Dictionary of Philosophy and Religion: Eastern and Western Thought*, 8th ed., (Atlantic Highlands, NJ: Humanities Press, 1980) 336–337, and William L. Reese, "Lenin, Vladimir Ilyich," 301.

[5] Edward Gibbon, *The Decline and Fall of the Roman Empire*, vol. III, (New York: Modern Library, 1983) 870.

[6] Merrill F. Unger, "Freedom," *Unger's Bible Dictionary*, 18th printing, (Chicago: Moody Press, 1972) 380.

[7] Warren Baker and Eugene Carpenter, "6862. צַר ṣar," *The Complete Word Study Dictionary, Old Testament*, (Chattanooga: AMG Publishers, 2003) 966-967.

[8] For a full discussion, please see: William Wilson, "Try, Trial," *Wilson's Old Testament Word Studies*, (Peabody: Hendrickson Publishers, 1990) 457, and John E. Hartley, "1972 צָרַף (ṣārap) smelt, refine, test," *Theological Workbook of the Old Testament*, R. Laird Harris, Gleason L. Archer, Jr., Bruce K Waktke, ed., vol. II, 2nd printing, (Chicago: Moody Press, 1981), 777-778.

⁹See: John N. Oswalt, "230 בָּחַן (bāḥan) to examine, try, prove," *Theological Workbook of the Old Testament*, R. Laird Harris, Gleason L. Archer, Jr., Bruce K Waktke, ed., vol. I, 2nd printing, (Chicago: Moody Press, 1981), 100, and Merrill F. Unger and William White, Jr., "To Test," "Nelson's Expository Dictionary of the Old Testament," in *Vine's Expository Dictionary of Biblical Words*, (Nashville: Thomas Nelson Publishers, 1985) 259-260.

¹⁰See: Spiros Zodhiates, "θλίψις," 736-739, and James Strong, "θλίψις," "Dictionary of Greek Words," *Strong's Exhaustive Concordance of the Bible*, (Iowa Falls: Riverside Book and Bible House, 19--?) 36, and Walter Bauer, "θλίψις," *A Greek-English Lexicon of the New Testament and Other Early Christian Literature*, F. Wilbur Gingrich and Frederick W. Danker, ed., 2nd rev. ed., (Chicago: University of Chicago Press, 1979) 362.

¹¹See: Spiros Zodhiates, "δοκίμιον," *The Complete Word Study Dictionary, New Testament*, rev. ed., (Chattanooga: AMG International, 1993) 476, and James Strong, "δοκίμιον," 24.

¹²See: James Strong, "δοκιμάζω," 24, Spiros Zodhiates, "δοκιμή," 475, and Walter Bauer, "δόκιμος," 203.

¹³Charles Pfeiffer and Everett Harrison, "Romans," *The Wycliffe Bible Commentary*, (Chicago: Moody Press, 1962) 1196.

Chapter Three

Chapter Three:
But We Glory in Tribulations Also

Hemmed In
It happened around the time when our youngest child left home, and we were "empty nesters" for the first time. Although my wife had been working, I could not find full-time work.

Then, I found an ad for a position that looked promising. The selected candidate would perform Christian research, writing, and publishing. Bible teaching, preaching, and developing adult spiritual growth curriculum and Christian service methodologies were job benefits as well.

My limited income, depleted savings, and plateaued professional endeavors led me to believe that this position, with its competitive salary and benefit package, was God's provision for the years of monetary and vocational hardship.

After I applied, my first interviewer described the position as being like an Old Testament watchman; the sentinel positioned on a high wall or tower overlooking the city, poised to alert inhabitants of any impending threats or danger.

The interviewer also confided that I impressed the company and my chances for hire were promising. I assumed my final interview would be a formality, and that I would begin a new career almost immediately.

When the company representative called to inform me they were looking for a "superstar," and not me, I felt extreme disappointment, pondering our uncertain future.

I felt helpless and constrained, having exhausted every known option, "hemmed in" with no relief in sight, pressured beyond my ability to cope.

I do not imply that my hardship was because of my faith in Jesus Christ. Neither can I compare my situation to the persecution and martyrdom the first-century Christians along with countless others have endured for Christ. In addition, I would be foolish to compare my problems to one moment of pain and suffering my Savior endured for me on Calvary's Cross.

Yet, I felt trapped in a very narrow place; pressed hard upon with no clear path to recovery or escape.

Our Divine Abnormality
Normal human responses to pressure are to fight, flee, or avoid (suppress). Christians use a different approach because Jesus, who is above all, instituted a higher standard that we are to follow,

> Blessed are those who are persecuted for righteousness' sake, for theirs is the kingdom of heaven. Blessed are you when they revile and persecute you, and say all kinds of evil against you falsely for My sake. Rejoice and be exceedingly glad, for

great is your reward in heaven, for so they persecuted the prophets who were before you. (Matthew 5:10-12)

Jesus Christ, who is above all, fulfilled the Law and introduced faith principles that separate and distinguish His Followers from the world. They also answer five essential questions,

1. How unshakable is my faith in Jesus Christ?
2. How important is my relationship with Jesus Christ and my love for God?
3. Since I have accepted Christ as my Savior, have I made Him my life's priority?
4. Am I willing to surrender all my worldly pursuits and possessions to Him?
5. Am I willing to obey God's Word (the Bible) as the supreme standard to govern my life?

Jesus tells us to turn the other cheek when challenged and not to resist evil. We also go the extra mile, extend ourselves to those in need, love our enemies, and forgive "seventy times seven" even if the offending person does not ask for forgiveness. (*cf.,* Matthew 5:38-48, 6:14-15, 18:21-22)

Instead of retaliation, we trust the Lord for justice, since vengeance is His, and He will repay. (Romans 12:19)

We are not masochists who derive pleasure from our pain and affliction. Neither do we want to live uncomfortably on earth. Instead, we follow Jesus Christ, who is our supreme role model for expressing certain remarkable characteristics our broken world deems as "abnormal."

Although we comprise the "Body of Christ" (1 Corinthians 12:27), we do not possess the Lord's moral and spiritual perfection. (If we were perfect, we'd have no need for a Savior.) Thus, we function at various levels of similitude in direct proportion to the level of spiritual and moral growth we have acquired over the years.

The Book of Acts offers a snapshot of the Christian Church's formation through the evangelistic work of the Apostles and other First Century Christians. Even the most casual reader must acknowledge the global spiritual, moral, social, and historical impact they made under the Lord's authority,

> And Jesus came and spoke to them, saying, "All authority has been given to Me in heaven and on earth. Go therefore and make disciples of all the nations, baptizing them in the name of the Father and of the Son and of the Holy Spirit, teaching them to observe all things that I have commanded you; and lo, I am with you always, even to the end of the age." Amen. (Matthew 28:18-20)

Acts begins with the Lord instructing His Followers to wait in Jerusalem until they receive the promise of the Holy Spirit. Then, it tells how, on the Day of Pentecost, the Holy Spirit descended on them while they were in the upper room, praying in one accord and waiting for God's manifestation to appear.

All at once, they proclaimed the message of Jesus' death, burial, and resurrection for the forgiveness of sins and the gift of eternal life under the Holy Spirit's power with great boldness, conviction, and courage. Almost overnight, the Gospel or "Good News" of Jesus Christ spread from Jerusalem to every remote corner of the world.

Miraculous signs and wonders followed these Spirit-powered men and women as they shared how they encountered the risen Christ. His tomb was empty; He was no longer dead, but alive and seated at the right hand of God. Their message "turned the world upside down." (Acts 17:6)

They encountered severe backlash, since they posed a threat to established faith groups and the Roman government where emperor worship was especially problematic since it mandated them to worship mortals as they would the Son of God. Violation often led to martyrdom, as this author observes,

> The refusal of all Christians to participate in [emperor worship] precipitated violent persecution, for the Christians consistently

objected to worshipping a human being. The polytheistic Romans, who could always add one more god to their list of deities, looked upon their refusal as a lack of proper recognition for the emperor and a distinctly unpatriotic attitude. Between these two viewpoints, there could be no reconciliation.[1]

When challenged today, we often become combatant and organize a protest campaign, but not so with these first-century Followers of Christ.

As the world ridiculed, criticized, persecuted, imprisoned, condemned, and martyred them, the Christian movement or The Way continued to grow and flourish. (*cf.*, Acts 9:2; 22:4)

People noticed how Jesus Christ was with them and that He gave them an "unnatural" response to hostility (*my emphasis*),

> Now when they saw the boldness of Peter and John, and perceived that they were uneducated and untrained men, *they marveled. And they realized that they had been with Jesus.* (Acts 4:13)

Further,

> So they departed from the presence of the council, *rejoicing that they were counted worthy to suffer shame for His name*. (Acts 5:41)

They did not evade pressure, run from conflict, hide from their persecutors, or conform to the secular societal demands their enemies had imposed on them.

They understood that our battle is not against physical foes, it's against sinister spiritual ones. (*cf.*, John 18:36, 1 Corinthians 10:3-6, Ephesians 6:10-18) Therefore, they welcomed trials and rejoiced through them, knowing that although we are in the world, we are not of it. As our Master suffered, we too must suffer, just as He forewarned,

> "If the world hates you, you know that it hated Me before it hated you. If you were of the world, the world would love its own. Yet because you are not of the world, but I chose you out of the world, therefore the world hates you. Remember the word that I said to you, 'A servant is not greater than his master.' If they persecuted Me, they will also persecute you. If they kept My word, they will keep yours also." (John 15:18-20)

They resolved to endure all things for their Savior. Standing firm in their convictions, they continued their normal, day-to-day activities by preaching, teaching, and living out their faith in Christ.

Each day they grew more resolute for Christ, convinced that whatever the outcome—good or bad—He was with them in Spirit. Yet, He was also preparing a glorious Heavenly home for them.

His shed blood and physical resurrection, along with the indwelling of the Holy Spirit, made their eternal destiny certain.

The essence of their impeccable Christian witness is that Jesus Christ, our Resurrected Savior, gives us complete victory over sin and death,

> These things I have spoken to you, that in Me you may have peace. In the world you will have tribulation; but be of good cheer, I have overcome the world. (John 16:33)

Also,

> But thanks be to God, who gives us the victory through our Lord Jesus Christ. Therefore, my beloved brethren, be steadfast, immovable, always abounding in the work of the Lord, knowing that your labor is not in vain in the Lord. (1 Corinthians 15:57-58)

We Glory in His Instruction and Direction

We have nothing to fear in this life or the next, because the blood of Jesus has abolished, rescinded, and annulled our enslavement to sin and death, and we will go to live in His glorious presence the very instant we die. (*cf.* 2 Corinthians 5:6-8, 1 John 3:6)

Our Lord will never leave or forsake us, even in uncertain times, so that whatever circumstance we face will not be beyond our capacity to endure it. (*cf.*, Deuteronomy 31:8, Psalm 23:4)

Although we will not win every battle or triumph in every situation, yet, God gives us the ability to rejoice or glory, Greek *"kauchaomai,"* (Strong-G2744),[2] in our tribulations.

We glory because the Eternal, Almighty Spirit of our living, reigning Lord and Savior—who subjected Himself to every human affliction and overcame—lives in us. We especially glory, because He has chosen us specifically to be His extraordinary representatives before a cynical, non-believing, and contemptuous world.

To show His power and teach a valuable lesson, Jesus once told His Disciples that a certain man's blindness would reveal "the works of God." (John 9:3) When He healed the man, it solidified His claim to be the Son of God.

The same loving and merciful God, who restored sight to the blind, can use tribulation to correct us and/or lead us in a direction He wants us to go.

Earlier, I shared how a company did not hire me. At the time, I could not understand why that door closed so quickly and emphatically. However, I soon learned that if I had followed that career path, I would have missed God's "greater good" for my entire family.

The Lord's "perfect will" was for my wife and me to be the primary caregivers for Mom and Grandma just before they passed away. It was a tough decision for us, but it was well worth the sacrifice.

Long after Dad had passed away, we remained a very close Christian family. Before meeting my wife, Mom was my best friend with Grandma as a very close second. After I married, my wife became my best friend. Although displaced, they adored my wife, and we all grew closer together as a result.

We moved across the country, where I became a prison chaplain. They were active members of their church, so we participated in church services together on those weekends when I was not working at the prison.

As their health failed, my wife and I, along with faithful hospice and in-home care staff, provided them with the constant, loving care they needed in their last days.

It was extremely difficult watching them decline, but the "good days" we shared through the many birthdays, holidays, vacation travel, etc., along with the inspiring stories they shared about their past, still evoke precious memories that will always warm and resonate within my heart.

God uses our trials to guide us toward achieving the noble behavior patterns that show we are His beloved sons and daughters,

> My son, do not despise the chastening of the Lord, Nor be discouraged when you are rebuked by Him; For whom the Lord loves He chastens, And scourges every son whom He receives. (Hebrews 12:5-6)

Although His chastening can be painful, it is always for our eternal benefit,

> Now no chastening seems to be joyful for the present, but painful; nevertheless, afterward it yields the peaceable fruit of righteousness to those who have been trained by it. (Hebrews 12:11)

Through trials, we can count it all joy as we collaborate with God in our spiritual completion,

> My brethren, count it all joy when you fall into various trials, knowing that the testing of your faith produces patience. But let patience have its perfect work, that you may be perfect and complete, lacking nothing. (James 1:2-4)

We are certain to encounter difficulty in this life, but as we do, we should never let our problems consume us. Instead, we should think about God's faithfulness and allow His joy to consume our hearts and minds.

When we glory in tribulations, we can focus on God's goodness. Over time, He replaces our fear and uncertainty with His peace and confidence. Each day, He proves to be our "refuge, strength, and ever-present help in trouble." (Psalm 46:1)

Ultimately, we grow more confident in the Lord who remains faithful always—even when we are not. Thus, we can "let go and let God" by surrendering our cares and circumstances to Him, because He cares for us and does all things well. (*cf.*, Mark 7:37, 2 Peter 5:7)

These Scriptures tell how it is beneficial to give the Lord control of our circumstances, knowing that He can and will provide for us,

> Commit your way to the Lord, Trust also in Him, And He shall bring it to pass. He shall bring forth your righteousness as the light, And your justice as the noonday. (Psalm 37:5-6)

> You will keep him in perfect peace, Whose mind is stayed on You, Because he trusts in You. (Isaiah 26:3)

> Be anxious for nothing, but in everything by prayer and supplication, with thanksgiving, let your requests be made known to God; and the peace of God, which surpasses all understanding, will

guard your hearts and minds through Christ Jesus. (Philippians 4:6-7)

Philippians 3:10 tells us we can experience the Lord's mighty power through our tribulations. We can glory because they connect us with Christ, whose goal is our perfection, as this author attests,

> What a difference between the proud stoicism of the heathen, who overcomes the misfortunes by haughty contempt and unfeeling indifferentism, and the Christian's gentle patience, forgiving love, and cheerful submission to the holy will of God, who ordered tribulation as a means and condition of moral perfection.[3]

The Lord guides us through our tribulations. Doubt and fear do not consume our lives as we glory, ever confident that He is fulfilling His plan that will glorify Him alone and benefit others and us. (*cf.*, Proverbs 18:24, 1 John 4:18)

Around the time I started in ministry, the Lord gave me a wonderful passage to remember,

> I am crucified with Christ: nevertheless I live; yet not I, but Christ liveth in me: and the life which I now live in the flesh I live by the faith of the Son of God, who loved me, and gave himself for me. Galatians 2:20 (AKJV)

In this chapter, we explored how we can glory in tribulation. The next chapter presents how our tribulation worketh patience.

Notes

[1] Merrill C. Tenney, "Emperor Worship," *New Testament Survey*, 7th printing, (Grand Rapids: Wm. B. Eerdmans Publishing, 1980) 67.

[2] See: James Strong, "καυχάομαι," "Dictionary of Greek Words," *Strong's Exhaustive Concordance of the Bible*, (Iowa Falls: Riverside Book and Bible House, 19--?) 41, and W.E. Vine, "Glory (to boast), Glorying," *An Expository Dictionary of New Testament Words*, in *Vine's Expository Dictionary of Biblical Words*, rev. ed. (Nashville: Thomas Nelson, 1985) 268.

[3] See: J.P. Lange, "Epistle of Paul to the Romans," *Commentary on the Holy Scriptures: Critical, Doctrinal and Homiletical*, Philip Schaff, trans., 7th ed., vol. 10, (Grand Rapids: Zondervan, 1980) 162.

Chapter Four

Chapter Four
Tribulation Worketh Patience

Unseen Forces at Work
It is impossible for us to comprehend God's mysteries and complexities. He is an Infinite Spirit whose ways and thoughts are loftier than anything we could ever imagine.

Yet, He patiently reveals Himself to us through Christ because He's not willing that we perish, but that we come to repentance, faith, and perfection in Him. (*cf.*, Psalm 147:5, Isaiah 55:9, 2 Peter 3:9)

Through His providence and preservation, He maintains a constant vigil over His creation so that we can "live, move, and have our being," and that in Him, "all things consist." (*cf.*, Acts 17:28, Colossians 1:17) One author describes God's providence this way,

> God is continually involved with all created things in such a way that he (1) keeps them existing and maintaining the properties with which he created them; (2) cooperates with created things in every action, directing their distinctive properties to cause them to act as they do; and (3) directs them to fulfill his purposes.[1]

My high school science teacher made physics and the natural sciences fascinating to me. I remember how we made invisible magnetic fields visible in class when we covered a magnet with a plain sheet of white paper and sprinkled iron filings on it. The electromagnetically-charged filings formed visible patterns that mirrored the unseen forces at work.

Then I learned how magnetically-charged metal filings were almost impossible to move when I saw the "mother lode" of all magnets at a local science fair. Extremely powerful, it looked like a thick horseshoe magnet, with about four inches separating its two magnetic poles.

It was "cool" to see how a powerful invisible force could suspend metal objects in mid-air to form a solid bridge between the two magnetic poles.

Jesus Christ is our only bridge to God. Before Him, all were imitators; after Him, all are pretenders. He is our source of life and vitality. He is the Vine, and we are His fruit-producing branches.

As our "mother lode" to spiritual and eternal life, He keeps us alive and vibrant as we abide in Him. Without Him, we are lifeless and will wither and die. (John 15:5)

Like a compass needle pointing north because of the magnetic forces at work, His Holy Spirit enables us to point the way toward Christ and eternal life to a broken and hurting world.

He is also our Almighty God, and His spiritual keeping power in us is far greater than our mortal strength to hold on to Him. One author relates our union with the Lord this way,

> Christ's omnipresence makes it possible for Him to be united to, and to be present in, each believer, as perfectly and fully as if that believer were the only one to receive Christ's fullness. ... each believer has the whole Christ with him as his source of strength, purity, life; so that each may say: Christ gives all his time and wisdom and care to me. Such a union as this lacks every element of instability. Once formed, the union is indissoluble. Many of the ties of earth are rudely broken,—not so with our union with Christ,—that endures forever. Since there is now an unchangeable and divine element in us, our salvation depends no longer upon our unstable wills, but upon Christ's purpose and power.[2]

Patience or perseverance is a byproduct of our faith, which God uses to strengthen our resolve to pursue Christ until we see Him in glory, as this author explains,

> [Perseverance] is due to the purpose of God, to the work of Christ, to the indwelling of the Holy Spirit, and to the primal source of all, the infinite, mysterious, and immutable love of God. We do not keep ourselves; we are kept by

the power of God, through faith unto salvation. (1 Peter 1:5)[3]

He has also given His angels the responsibility to comfort and watch over us throughout our spiritual pilgrimage as well.

Abiding Under in Complete Surrender
Through our tribulations, God invigorates our spiritual depth, and His almighty power preserves our spiritual well-being. Just as fire refines precious metals, God uses tribulation to refine our patient endurance so that we face our challenges with bravery and fortitude.

The Greek word "*hupomone,*" (Strong-G5281),[4] translated as patience, combines two Greek words "*hupo,*" under, and "*meno,*" to abide to convey remaining patient, enduring, being steadfast in our resolve, particularly in our Christian faith.

To "abide under" means to surrender our will to Christ while we humbly and patiently endure by remaining steadfast in our service to Him.

It must be pointed out that God never intends us to "abide under" the threat of danger or physical harm. We must address those circumstances carefully, with prayer, counseling, and appropriate intervention(s) on a case-by-case basis.

We are priceless commodities made in His image, and He wants us to practice self-care by seeking proper guidance when there is a threat of violence, exploitation, and/or abuse.[5]

Yet, we can trust the Lord to give us the wisdom and discernment to avoid situations that would imperil others or us as we grow into the level of Christ-likeness He advocates in His Word,

> Let this mind be in you which was also in Christ Jesus, who, being in the form of God, did not consider it robbery to be equal with God, but made Himself of no reputation, taking the form of a bondservant, and coming in the likeness of men. And being found in appearance as a man, He humbled Himself and became obedient to the point of death, even the death of the cross. (Philippians 2:5-8)

Patient endurance requires our complete surrender to the Lord. This is most difficult since it forces us to overcome our greatest internal enemy—pride. One author explores the freedom we have as we submit ourselves to Christ,

> What freedom corresponds to submission? It is the ability to lay down the terrible burden of always needing to get our own way. The obsession to demand that things go the way we want them to go is one of the greatest bondages in human society today. ... In the discipline of submission we are released to drop the matter, to forget it. ... Only

submission can free us sufficiently to enable us to distinguish between genuine issues and stubborn self-will.[6]

It is the Lord's job to lead us. It is our job to follow Him by trusting His leadership and obeying His sovereignty, as this hymn conveys,

>Trust and Obey[7]
>John H. Sammis
>(1846-1919)

When we walk with the Lord in the light of His Word, what a glory He sheds on our way! While we do His good will, He abides with us still, And with all who will trust and obey.

Not a shadow can rise, not a cloud in the skies, But His smile quickly drives it away; Not a doubt nor a fear, not a sigh nor a tear, Can abide while we trust and obey.

Not a burden we bear, not a sorrow we share, but our toil He doth richly repay; not a grief nor a loss, not a frown nor a cross, But is blest if we trust and obey.

But we never can prove the delights of His love Until all on the altar we lay; For the favor He shows and the joy He bestows Are for them who will trust and obey.

Then in fellowship sweet we will sit at His feet, Or we'll walk by His side in the way; what He says we will do, where He sends we will go, never fear, only trust and obey.

Refrain:
Trust and obey, for there's no other way
To be happy in Jesus, but to trust and obey.

Once a very difficult trial led me to consider quitting my job, but a spiritually-discerning counselor advised me to stay there because it was "where God planted me."

After praying and seeking the Lord, I stayed. Not long afterwards, it became clear that my staying brought about God's glory and my co-workers' benefit (as well as mine).

Gradually, I learned how to love and serve my co-workers, as unto the Lord. Over time, the conflicts I had grew into non-issues. In addition, the company recognized our department for its congeniality and productivity.

That experience taught me how God can position us to be His "salt and light" and become His loving hands in the most unlikely places. (Matthew 5:13-14)

I also learned that I would have missed a tremendous blessing had I left, because I developed lifelong associations with those I had strained relations with initially.

Surrendering to Christ frees us to trust and obey Him, knowing that we will receive far greater benefits than all the loss or distress our problems will cause us, just as the Scriptures attest,

> And we know that all things work together for good to those who love God, to those who are the called according to His purpose. (Romans 8:28)

Managing Our Emotions
To help us avoid falling prey to our feelings by blaming God, and giving up when tribulation occurs, Jesus warns us to count the cost before committing our lives to Him,

> For which of you, intending to build a tower, does not sit down first and count the cost, whether he has enough to finish it—lest, after he has laid the foundation, and is not able to finish, all who see it begin to mock him, saying, 'This man began to build and was not able to finish'? Or what king, going to make war against another king, does not sit down first and consider whether he is able with ten thousand to meet him who comes against him with twenty thousand? Or else, while the other is still a great way off, he sends a

delegation and asks conditions of peace. (Luke 14:28-32)

Managing our emotions can help us avoid projecting our joy/sorrow on God (e.g., God's good when things are going well, and He's bad when things are not going well). In our broken world, "bad" and "good" things often happen without rhyme or reason.

Thus, expecting God to give us wealth, success, comfort, health, or ease because we live for Christ is an unrealistic and unhealthy expectation we must not adopt as our foundation of faith.

Although the Lord will provide for and protect His Children without question, it is both irrational and childish for us to treat our Creator as if He is our personal genie to grant our every desire upon demand.

All the Lord's promises in Christ are "yes and amen." (2 Corinthians 1:20) Yet, He is God, and sometimes His "best" answer for us is no.

It is at these times when we need to replace our "rose-colored glasses" with an honest assessment of our motives, desires, and intent, and conform to His will.

Ultimately, we must trust God to perform His perfect will for us, in us, and through us for that precise moment in time, by yielding to Him as did our Lord at Gethsemane (_my emphasis_),

> And He said, "Abba, Father, all things are possible for You. Take this cup away from Me; <u>*nevertheless, not what I will, but what You will.*</u>" (Mark 14:36)

More often than not, our best plans clash with the Lord's will. As this occurs, we must learn to yield to His will to "do justly, love mercy, and walk humbly" with Him in perfect surrender. (Micah 6:8) He will use this attitude in us to foster a proper faith development.

Departing the Faith
Jesus established certain protocols for effective, sacrificial Christian living,

> Then He said to them all, "If anyone desires to come after Me, let him deny himself, and take up his cross daily, and follow Me. For whoever desires to save his life will lose it, but whoever loses his life for My sake will save it. For what profit is it to a man if he gains the whole world, and is himself destroyed or lost? For whoever is ashamed of Me and My words, of him the Son of Man will be ashamed when He comes in His own glory, and in His Father's, and of the holy angels." (Luke 9:23-26)

In His parable of the Great Supper, (Luke 14:16-20, 24), Jesus tells of the fate of those who reassess their commitment to Him and cite marriage, family, or property issues.

There will always be those who contend that the Christian life is too hard.

Many will tell of a personal tragedy or deep hurt that caused them to rethink their faith in the Lord. We will face personal tragedy in this life. One author tells of certain pressures that have caused many to depart the faith in this new millennium,

> The future is even more frightening for this generation inundated with threats of global terrorism. This group, not unlike previous generations, is seeking answers. But with so much information in the palms of their hands, profound questions of life and the future are even more numerous and pressing.[8]

Interpersonal conflict resulting in flight or avoidance is another reason for abandoning our faith, as these authors explain,

> Avoidance, the most commonly used style of conflict management, reflects the belief that it is impossible to both accomplish our personal goals and maintain relationships while in conflict. ...The basic strategy of avoidance is to withdraw, avoid, suppress, and deny the existence of conflict. A person using this style is unassertive, neither pursuing his or her

own interests in the situation, nor supporting others in achieving theirs. This person will not cooperate in defining the conflict, seeking solution, or in carrying it out.[9]

Whatever the reason for departure, Jesus presents this phenomenon in His Parable of the Sower.

There, He shows how the message of salvation can come to us as "seed planted on good soil" that yields an abundant crop. (*cf.*, Matthew 13:3-9, Mark 4:3-9, Luke 8:4-8)

However, He also shows, through the seed falling by the wayside, the seed falling stony ground, and the seed falling among thorns, how a verbal profession alone will not guarantee our fellowship with Christ and God, and when He returns, He will banish them from His presence,

> Not everyone who says to Me, 'Lord, Lord,' shall enter the kingdom of heaven, but he who does the will of My Father in heaven. Many will say to Me in that day, 'Lord, Lord, have we not prophesied in Your name, cast out demons in Your name, and done many wonders in Your name?' And then I will declare to them, 'I never knew you; depart from Me, you who practice lawlessness!' (Matthew 7:21-23)

John the Apostle tells how those who profess Christ without committing their lives to Him will abandon their faith,

> They went out from us, but they were not of us; for if they had been of us, they would no doubt have continued with us: but they went out, that they might be made manifest that they were not all of us. (1 John 2:19)

As a crowd turned away from Jesus, He looked at His Twelve Disciples and asked if they were going to leave Him as well. Peter replies,

> Lord, to whom shall we go? Thou hast the words of eternal life. And we believe and are sure that thou art that Christ, the Son of the living God. John 6:68–69 (AKJV)

We can form an unbreakable bond with Jesus because He is the way, truth, and life, and no one comes to the Father except through Him. (John 14:6)

Enduring Triumphantly

The Bible offers us keys for sacrificial living that are well pleasing to our King,

> I beseech you therefore, brethren, by the mercies of God, that you present your bodies a living sacrifice, holy, acceptable to God, which is your reasonable service. And do not be conformed to this world,

but be transformed by the renewing of your mind, that you may prove what is that good and acceptable and perfect will of God. (Romans 12:1-2)

God gave the very best He had to redeem us, and the very least He expects from us is to be "living sacrifices" for Him each day; not conformed to worldly standards, but transformed by His mighty power in us.

Our profession of faith in Christ presumes a personal commitment that brings about spiritual transformation.

Thus, we who profess *and believe* in Christ will endure. (Romans 10:9-10) He is our hope, strength, and victory as we progress toward our glorious Heavenly home.

Because Christ persevered and triumphed, we have the victory as the Holy Spirit sustains and comforts us. (John 14:16-18)

The Apostle John was the last remaining Disciple. He lived with the Lord for three years along with his fellow Disciples. He witnessed Pentecost and the New Testament church.

Despite his exile and the tyrannical Roman persecution, John persevered, and we can, too, just as Jesus predicted,

> Holy Father, keep through thine own name those whom thou hast given me, that they may be one, as we are. While I was with them in the world, I kept them in thy name: those that thou gavest me I have kept, and none of them is lost, but the son of perdition; that the scripture might be fulfilled. John 17:11b–12 (AKJV)

We may doubt the Lord's goodness. Nevertheless, He has not abandoned us. Our tribulations do not negate God's love, grace, and mercy, neither do they "prove" His desertion. His Spirit strengthens our resolve to seek first His Kingdom and righteousness, and trust Him for the results. (Matthew 6:33)

The toils and disappointments we face along the way serve as reminders that we occupy a broken world that juxtaposes the glorious, eternal home He's preparing for us.

There, all our earthly pain, toil, and suffering will vanish the very instant we see our Lord and Savior, Jesus Christ, in His full majestic splendor, just as Revelation 21:4 tells us,

> And God will wipe away every tear from their eyes; there shall be no more death, nor sorrow, nor crying. There shall be no more pain, for the former things have passed away.

We will also understand each trial and tribulation we experienced in life as everything will become as clear as crystal, just as He promises,

> For we know in part and we prophesy in part. But when that which is perfect has come, then that which is in part will be done away. ... For now we see in a mirror, dimly, but then face to face. Now I know in part, but then I shall know just as I also am known. (1 Corinthians 13:9-10, 12)

Our patient endurance under trial brings about God's approval as this author relates,

> It is the condition of approval, whose subjective expression is the consciousness of being sealed; Eph. 2:13. ...The word is used metonymically for the result of trial, i.e., approbation, or that which is proved worthy of approbation. It is tried integrity, a state of mind, which has stood the test.[10]

Another author frames our patient endurance this way,

> And patience experience; full proof, by trial, of the truth of our religion, the solidity of our Christian state, and the faithfulness of our God. In such cases, we have the opportunity of putting our religion to the test, and by every such test, it receives the deeper sterling stamp. The Apostle uses here also a metaphor taken

from the purifying, refining, and testing of silver and gold.[11]

We can glory in tribulation, putting our faith to the test each day through patient endurance, knowing that God is with us and is trustworthy.

As we bear under each trial successfully, we reveal how our Christian faith is authentic and relevant as it passes every successive test we encounter.

In this chapter, we explored how tribulation worketh patience. In the next chapter, we will see how patience worketh experience.

Notes

[1]Wayne A. Grudem, "God's Providence," *Systematic Theology: An Introduction to Biblical Doctrine,* (Leicester, England; Grand Rapids, Michigan: Inter-Varsity Press; Zondervan Pub. House, 2004) 315.

[2]Augustus H. Strong, "Union with Christ," *Systematic Theology,* 31st ed., (Valley Forge: Judson Press, 1976) 801.

[3]Charles Hodge, "Effects of Faith," *Systematic Theology,* 3rd printing, vol. III, (Peabody: Hendrickson, 2003) 113.

[4]Spiros Zodhiates, "ὑπομονή," *The Complete Word Study Dictionary, New Testament,* rev. ed., (Chattanooga: AMG International, 1993) 1425, and W.E. Vine, "Patience, Patient, Patiently," *An Expository Dictionary of New Testament Words,* in *Vine's Expository Dictionary of Biblical Words,* rev. ed. (Nashville: Thomas Nelson, 1985) 462.

[5]Contact a qualified professional, Christian counselor, social/community service agency, or law enforcement for appropriate referral and/or crisis intervention.

[6]Richard J. Foster, "The Discipline of Submission," *Celebration of Discipline: The Path to Spiritual Growth,* (San Francisco: Harper & Row, 1978) 97.

[7]John H. Sammis, "Trust and Obey," *The New Church Hymnal,* Ralph Carmichael, et al., ed., (Newbury Park: Lexicon Music, 1976) 327.

[8]Alex McFarland and Jason Jimenez, "Hope for a Generation," *Abandoned Faith: Why Millennials are Walking Away and How You Can Lead Them Home,* (Carol Stream: Tyndale House, 2017) 121.

[9]L. Randolph Lowery, J.D., and Richard W. Meyers, "Responding to Conflict," *Conflict Management and*

Counseling: Resources for Christian Counseling, Gary R. Collins, ed., vol. 29, (Dallas: Word, 1991) 30-31.

[10]J.P. Lange, "Epistle of Paul to the Romans," *Commentary on the Holy Scriptures: Critical, Doctrinal and Homiletical*, Philip Schaff, trans., 7th ed., vol. 10, (Grand Rapids: Zondervan, 1980) 162.

[11]Adam Clarke, "A General Survey of the Epistle to the Romans," *Clarke's Commentary*, new ed., vol. VI, (New York: Abingdon Press, 19—?) 66.

Chapter Five

Chapter Five
Patience Worketh Experience

Making the Grade
I was sitting at my dining room table staring out the window at the trees that lined the street bordering our condominium complex.

The peaceful ambiance of that beautiful fall day would have been calming under normal circumstances, but I was in a fierce internal struggle to draft, edit, and submit my dissertation to meet the graduation requirements within the next few weeks.

I was feeling overwhelmed by the enormity of the moment. It was December, and I had not written my paper. I had an outline and research notes, but I did not have the wherewithal to condense, synthesize, and quantify my research, ministry practicum, and faith experience in the required scholarly format to that point.

I started internalizing the skeptics and naysayers who said I could not complete the program; maybe they were right after all?

Maybe this "poor black kid from the projects" does not have what it takes to earn a doctorate. Several of my classmates left the program; why not be like them?

Over twenty years had passed since I entered college. I pondered how my quitting at this stage would affect my wife, children, and parents, who have supported and encouraged me throughout and planned to attend my graduation.

I also considered the time and money I invested in tuition, books, attending classes, writing research papers, training volunteers, compiling data, conducting my case study, and attending weekly meetings with my committee chairperson.

I realized that quitting at this stage was not an option. It was time to close this chapter in my life and say goodbye to the physical, emotional, and financial pressures it caused us.

Yet, I was in a predicament that was beyond my acumen, aptitude, and resources to resolve successfully. In my moment of despair, I cried out to the Lord God and asked Him to do (in me and through me), what I could not do for myself.

At that moment, the Lord gave me the Scripture I needed to contextualize my research and its findings. Then shortly thereafter, He led me to an editor and a professional printer who helped me prepare my work for its formal presentation.

My graduation ceremony was a most memorable event, with family and well-wishers shouting as the seminary president presented me over the PA system, along with the other graduates.

After the announcement, while still on stage, I presented my wife with roses, to show my appreciation for her years of sacrifice and support.

Praise the Lord, we made the grade!

Making the grade epitomizes the Greek word we translate as experience *"dokime,"* (Strong-G1382),[1] showing how something has completed the test and has been approved.

We endure this Christian race to become Christ-like. We complete it, because we love the Lord and want Him to congratulate us in person when we cross the finish line.

However, along the way, our completion becomes more than mere proof of our genuineness. It also becomes an opportunity for God to imprint His character and personality in us so that we pass His final grade successfully—*Christ-likeness!*

Here is how one person views this process,

> The heart's experience of justification must be put to proof, in which it becomes the historically established experience of life. Steadfastness in such proof results inwardly in sealing by the Holy Spirit ... and outwardly in the establishment of the Christian in the character of his new nature. ...This is ethically connected with the fact that, by the test of tribulation and steadfastness, a purifying process has

taken place, by which a separation of the most combustible material has been effected.[2]

Partnering With God
The Born Again experience frees us from sin's dominion. In this condition, the Lord can teach us how to subdue our carnal thoughts, intents, and desires so that we cause no harm to others and ourselves.

Because God's holiness mandates ours, we join Him in the process of our spiritual and moral character development through sanctification, which is both active and passive.

It is passive as God uses His Holy Spirit to complete His good work within us. (Philippians 1:6)

He shapes us into Christ's moral and spiritual image by revealing to us things pertaining to Jesus Christ and solid Christian living while imparting God's holiness within our hearts, as this author observes,

> There is no holiness in any human heart until the Holy Spirit produces it. Implanted in regeneration and developed in sanctification ... he renovates the soul, purifies it, and prepares it for heaven.[3]

Another author frames the Spirit's work this way,

The Spirit also sustains relations to us, and performs offices which none but a person can sustain or perform. He is our teacher, sanctifier, comforter, and guide. He governs every believer who is led by the Spirit, and the whole church. He calls, as he called Barnabas and Saul, to the work of the ministry, or to some special field of labor. Pastors or bishops are made overseers by the Holy Ghost.[4]

He also illuminates the Bible to us so that we can understand God's plan for us individually. He serves as God's "seal" to guarantee our eternal salvation, and He helps us to pray when our words cannot express our burdens to God adequately.

In addition, He supplies us with the spiritual gifts, abilities, comfort, and strength we need to complete our Christian pilgrimage successfully.

Our sanctification becomes active when we surrender to the Lord daily by forming and performing the ascetic habits of Bible study, prayer, regular corporate worship, fellowship with other believers, financial giving (tithes and offerings), and Christian service that enhance our spiritual and moral vitality.

Over time, we learn to practice characteristics that resemble His holiness consistently, while casting off those problematic traits and habits that resemble this evil world.

We will never become perfect in this life. But as we grow spiritually, we can learn how to replace our desires for the visible, temporal, and earthly with a yearning for the godly, unseen, and eternal as the Scriptures admonish us,

> While we do not look at the things which are seen, but at the things which are not seen. For the things which are seen are temporary, but the things which are not seen are eternal. (Corinthians 4:8-10, 16-18)

Now spiritually alive, we commit to being His abundant living, spiritually transformed, and graciously redeemed sons and daughters, who are "more than conquerors" and can "do all things through Jesus Christ who strengthens us." (Romans 8:37, Philippians 4:13)

Just as Jesus surrendered to the will of His Father, we, too, can yield to God's will by putting on His holy image, as this author explains,

> [Sanctification] is a precious reality, involving holiness of heart, which leads to holiness of life. It has its origin in regeneration, for regeneration is the beginning of holiness in the soul. ... Now, while regeneration implants the germ of holiness in the heart, sanctification is the unfolding of that germ. This being the case, it follows that regeneration and

sanctification are essentially the same in nature, and may be regarded as two parts of the moral process by which depraved man is restored to the image of God.[5]

This will allow us to grow "in favor with God and humanity" as did our Lord. (Luke 2:52) It is possible to acquire God's wonderful character in our process of moral and spiritual growth.

Displaying God's Character

Character is the collection of traits that reveal someone's distinct nature or identity. We are subjects of the Eternal Monarch who wants us to display His impeccable character before a sinful and broken world. Here is how one author describes the formation of godly character,

> Character is caught as much as it is taught. Our natural inclinations, or sensitivities, are the raw material for developing character. These can be nurtured and directed toward the good, or restrained and distorted. The difference will come from the habits we form as well as the influence of our social worlds. A common theme of the ethics of character is that the actions we perform will in turn form us. Character emerges from the habits we establish which reflect the beliefs, ideals, and images of life that we have internalized as a result of the influence of the communities in which we live, especially the people within those

communities who have captured our imaginations.⁶

Although we cannot live out God's self-existence, omnipotence, omnipresence, and omniscience, we can show His selfless love, truthfulness, and faithfulness.

God's Selfless Love and Our Compassion
Love is an emotional expression we can have toward another person or object. Thus, we can love our job, our homes, classical music, fine cuisine, etc.

Webster's defines it as our "strong affection for another arising out of kinship or personal ties; to hold dear; cherish."⁷

Selfless love describes God's deliberate choice to accomplish what is *always* in our best interest. Jesus articulates this transcendent concept when He commanded a new love paradigm (<u>*my emphasis*</u>),

> A new commandment I give unto you, That ye love one another; <u>*as I have loved you*</u>, that ye also love one another. By this shall all men know that ye are my disciples, if ye have love one to another. (John 13:34-35)

In Jesus' new model, He uses the Greek word "*agape*," (Strong NT26)⁸ to show God's exquisite character when He made the deliberate choice to extend a pure, selfless affection toward a fallen humanity through the redeeming work of Christ,

> In this the love of God was manifested toward us, that God has sent His only begotten Son into the world, that we might live through Him. In this is love, not that we loved God, but that He loved us and sent His Son to be the propitiation for our sins. (1 John 4:9-10)

We were God's adversaries. Yet, He demonstrated a perfect love toward us. In like manner, we can extend ourselves toward other people with genuine care, concern, reconciliation, and forgiveness—even when the other person is an enemy,

> You have heard that it was said, 'You shall love your neighbor and hate your enemy.' But I say to you, love your enemies, bless those who curse you, do good to those who hate you, and pray for those who spitefully use you and persecute you . . . For if you love those who love you, what reward have you? . . . and if you greet your brethren only, what do you do more than others? ... Therefore you shall be perfect, just as your Father in heaven is perfect. (Matthew 5:43-48)

It is easy for us to love when someone reciprocates it. Relationships fail when we cannot show love that covers a multitude of faults.

Love is a difficult yet practical choice that allows us to relinquish our pride and anger to extend benevolence and forgiveness, as this author illustrates,

> To forgive someone is to admit our limitations. God's given us only one piece of life's jigsaw puzzle. Only God has the cover of the box. To forgive someone is to display reverence. Forgiveness is not saying the one who hurt you was right. Forgiveness is stating that God is fair and he will do what is right. After all, don't we have enough things to do without trying to do God's work too? [9]

Death is the ultimate price that one can pay to show love, and God, through Christ, did that for us at Calvary. His divine love extends mercy and forgiveness to all people everywhere. We emulate God's perfect love when we forgive wrongdoings, show mercy, and extend goodwill.

Mercy is not a popular subject, although we need to express it in today's world. Because when someone offends us, our first response is retribution. However, when God's offended, His is a very different response through Christ,

> If we confess our sins, He is faithful and just to forgive us our sins and to cleanse us from all unrighteousness. 1 John 1:9

Instead of judgment, He forgives us and keeps no record of our sinful past. Psalm 103:12 tells us He removes our sins from us as far as the east is separated from the west.

We deserved eternal judgment and condemnation. Yet, His selfless love prompted Him to restore us imposing no restriction. Mercy says that we have no probation period whereby we "earn" God's favor.

Nothing can separate us from God. Neither can anything in our past make us guilty before Him. Thus, we can reflect His mercy as our being prime benefactors. (Romans 8:35-39)

Motivated by God's selfless love, our compassion becomes a viable and attractive alternative to all forms of love outside of Christ. It encompasses the "most excellent way" outlined in 1 Corinthians 13 (the *Love Chapter*).

Patient and kind, it's always at work seeking opportunities to show kindness. It is not jealous, boastful, proud, or rude. It is not possessive or irritable. It does not concern itself with what the recipient can do to "deserve" it, nor does it demand its own way.

It keeps no record of wrongs, and it rejoices when truth prevails. It never gives up, never loses faith, but is hopeful and enduring.

Our Lord lived it from the beginning of time, and He will complete this perfect work in us. Thus, love reveals the unselfish heart of God to us, just as 1 John 4:7-8 tells us,

> Beloved, let us love one another, for love is of God; and everyone who loves is born of God and knows God. He who does not love does not know God, for God is love.

When asked to name the greatest Commandment, the Lord answered, in Matthew 22:37, it was to love God. We can love God, because He loves us, and He created us for eternal fellowship.

We cannot disregard loving our neighbors and ourselves (Matthew 22:39), but our love for God must define us, as this author summarizes,

> To love God this completely we must come apart from the daily press of life and spend time alone with God, reading His Word, meditating upon it, and praying to Him. We are to love God with the totality of our being, and this cannot be done on the run. We must pause, quiet our hearts, and listen for the "still small voice of God." If we will love God in our private watch with all our heart, soul, and mind, then we will be able to go into the marketplace and love Him there, also, with all of our strength.[10]

Loving God means we yearn to spend quality time with Him daily. We also read His Word and obey it. We do not worship other "idols" or flippantly use His name in vain.

When we commune with Him in prayer, our communication is two way. We share our concerns and tell Him how much we love Him, and we listen to Him as He speaks to us by His Word and Spirit.

We show our love by serving His church and others in need. We refrain from lying, cheating, or coveting others. Instead, seek their best interest as if we were doing it to Christ Himself,

> Assuredly, I say to you, inasmuch as you did it to one of the least of these My brethren, you did it to Me. (Matthew 25:40)

When we express God's love, we can live right in the eyes of God and humanity. In God's eyes, we are His obedient Children who show His marvelous character. To humanity, we reveal God's redeeming love and testify that we belong to His Son, Jesus Christ.

God's Truthfulness and Our Honesty
God is the embodiment of all that is true. This writer describes God's truthfulness or veracity,

> Veracity is that perfection in God which renders all his judgments according to

truth, which prompts him to say what is true, and which makes it impossible for him to lie.[11]

We reflect God's truthfulness or veracity in our honesty; the noble lifestyle we have gained through habitual practice to show how our character and conduct are consistent and firm.

We use words like integrity, sincerity, authentic, reputable, and valid to describe people who show this character trait. Our conduct offers meaning and relevance to our Christian witness as we demonstrate a higher, sincere, and forthright contrasting quality to negate and refute the dishonesty of others around us.

Christ is our supreme example, who consistently performed honesty with exceptional spiritual and moral maturity. Likewise, we emulate His honesty in our interactions with God and the world around us.

Before we came to Christ, we were villainous and gave no thought of what we said or how we acted. Now that He is in us, we are virtuous and are concerned about our conduct and character.

He replaces our deceit with sincerity and our duplicity with integrity. We keep our word and speak the truth in love. We do not use the truth as a weapon to inflict harm, but as a tool for healing, instruction, and edification. (Ephesians 4:15)

Honesty is the fundamental characteristic that completes a person who can establish and nurture trust that result in positive working and learning relationships.

We also nurture safety as we keep promises and not make excuses for our failings. We want to be true to Christ, our role model, by living out a similar lifestyle consistently.

As honest citizens, we do not cheat on taxes or exams, neither do we plagiarize; we turn in honest/accurate reports at school and/or work. We obey the laws of the land (except those that contradict Scripture and moral conscience), and we honor and pray for our civic leaders regardless of party affiliation.

Not just truthful, our God is faithful in all things, which helps us to become His reliable and dependable Children.

God's Faithfulness and Our Reliability
When we speak of God's faithfulness, we affirm that God is able to fulfill His promises, as one author observes,

> In God's faithfulness we have the sure ground of confidence that he will perform what his love has led him to promise to those who obey the gospel. Since his promises are based, not upon what we are or have done, but upon what Christ is and has done, our defects and errors do not

> invalidate them, so long as we are truly penitent and believing ... God's faithfulness also ensures a supply for all the real wants of our being, both here and hereafter, since these wants are implicit promises of him who made us.[12]

Each day, we allow the Lord to strengthen our moral fiber so that our words and actions are consistent. Just as He is faithful about keeping His promises, likewise, we grow to keep ours, since committing to someone gives them (God or people) the permission to expect us to fulfill our obligations.

When the Disciples fell asleep at the Garden of Gethsemane, Jesus noted that our "spirits are willing, but the flesh (body) is weak." (*cf.*, Matthew 26:41, Mark 14:38) Thus, He has given us His Spirit to help us form habits of watching our words (what we promise) so that we can fulfill them—especially since we are Followers of Jesus Christ, the Supreme Promise Keeper.

By every standard, we should not allow our "mouths to cause our flesh to sin" (Ecclesiastes 5:6), and thus give someone ammunition to consider us unreliable. The "who we are when no one is watching" should speak and act consistently and appropriately. Then, we, too, can be faithful and true like our Blessed Redeemer,

> Now I saw heaven opened, and behold, a white horse. And He who sat on him was

called Faithful and True, and in righteousness He judges and makes war. (Revelation 19:11)

As God's stewards, He blesses us to help people in need, and He demands our faithful compliance.

In the home, everyone is safe from sexual, physical, and emotional abuse. We are dependable stewards of the precious gift of family members that God has given us in the home. Thus, we offer encouragement, nurturing, training, and support instead of disrespectful or insulting words and actions.

Faithful and reliable, we love our spouses as we share in the responsibilities of maintaining a Christ-centered home where each member has well-defined roles and clear boundaries to model truth, sincerity, and reliability before the world.

Our reliability as caregivers helps our children understand the consequences of poor choices and wrong behavior through appropriate discipline. We also expose and advocate Christian values to our children while they are young. (Proverbs 22:6, Ecclesiastes 12:1)

This helps them develop constructive pursuits and devote themselves to the Lord through religious or secular vocations. It also trains the next generation to become safe, respectful, and sociable members of a civil society.

Even during prolonged or end-of-life illnesses, we can be faithful and reliable as we take on the responsibility of providing care for our ailing parents.

In so doing, we not just show our love and appreciation for all that they have done for us—to make us who we are—we also fulfill God's command to honor them. (Exodus 2:12)

In social and religious gatherings, we never use our power, position, or influence to cause harm. Instead, we extend ourselves to other races, cultures, ages, genders, and social statuses. We celebrate diversity and synergy by abstaining from bigotry and discrimination.

Reliability also means that we yield to authority, follow instructions, and do not express petty sentiments toward others. We do not defraud our employers through malingering, neither do we use the company's equipment/resources for personal gain, and we do not use company time for catching up on social media or non-work related reading.[13]

At school, we abstain from binge drinking, exhibitionism, sexual promiscuity, and hazing that will endanger others and ourselves. We respect our administrators, teachers, and colleagues. We are amenable with our peers, and we protect the school equipment that's been assigned to us.

In every way possible, we stand firm on the Bible, the lamp for our feet and the light for our path, as spiritual and moral ambassadors for Christ. (*cf.*, Psalm 119:105, Luke 19:13, Ephesians 6:13)

A Biblical Response
We are God's "salt" and "light," to interject spice and flavor into a drab and morbid world through noble character alternatives that impede the moral and spiritual degeneration of our society.

With each successive day of walking in the Spirit, making no provisions to fulfill fleshly lusts, (*cf.*, Romans 13:14, Galatians 5:16), we learn it is far better to live in harmony with God, our neighbors, and ourselves than to be slaves to sin and our selfish cravings.

Over time, we can find joy in establishing and fostering a viable relationship with God as well as "safe" relationships with others who may or may not share our gender, age, race, or culture.

Viable means that we are "straight up" with God by not making excuses to cover our sin and failings.

We do not try to impress God with our pedigree and stories, neither do we try to fool Him with our masks and deflections. He knows our thoughts, actions, weaknesses and strengths, motives, and intentions.

He loves us and craves an honest fellowship with us where we can tell Him our troubles, doubts, fears, hurts, shortcomings, wants, needs, and aspirations. Then He can heal and strengthen us properly while guiding us along His perfect path.

We grow to discover that just as we are safe in God's presence, others can be safe in ours. Safe means we refrain from seeking to establish predator/victim associations with others. Jesus says that we will pay a terrible price if we victimize others to satisfy our own debauched cravings,

> Then He said to the disciples, "It is impossible that no offenses should come, but woe to him through whom they do come! It would be better for him if a millstone were hung around his neck, and he were thrown into the sea, than that he should offend one of these little ones." (Luke 17:1-2)

Instead, we display affirming words, gestures, and actions that show our genuine concern for the other person's dignity and well-being.

This allows us to function in society, free from the inclination to impose our repulsive "baggage" on others to gratify our malevolent inner cravings.

- We do not practice "Pharisee-ism" as God's pompous and "holier than thou" special gifts to the world. None of us has arrived at perfection, and more than likely, we are serving our pride instead of serving Christ.

- We are not Christian Libertines who live for Christ and the world simultaneously. Since no person can serve two masters, typically our flesh prevails at the expense of our stellar Christian witness.

- We are not "Cynical Saints" who avoid all social activity and common associations because we see evil in everything and everyone but never in us. God wants us to make a positive impact by actively serving wherever He sends us at home or abroad.

- We are not "Rapture Watchers" consumed with eschatology or Christ's return and final events only. None of us knows the exact day or time our Lord will return. Yet, He mandates us not to be hermits but to share His love and great salvation through our words and gestures until He returns for us.

We seek to live a "balanced" Christian life, where we think, speak, and act with a mind to honor God while facilitating positive outcomes for other people and ourselves consistently, since we will have to account for our conduct and character,

> For we must all appear before the judgment seat of Christ, that each one may receive the things done in the body,

> according to what he has done, whether good or bad. (2 Corinthians 5:10)

Making the grade shows God's efficacy to purify our old nature to make us new creatures suitable for Heaven so that when He returns, those of us who complete this Christian marathon will receive His glorious commendation,

> Do you not know that those who run in a race all run, but one receives the prize? Run in such a way that you may obtain it. And everyone who competes for the prize is temperate in all things. Now they do it to obtain a perishable crown, but we for an imperishable crown. Therefore I run thus: not with uncertainty. Thus I fight: not as one who beats the air. But I discipline my body and bring it into subjection, lest, when I have preached to others, I myself should become disqualified. (I Corinthians 9:24-27)

Trials are inevitable, and as we endure them, we can look to God's Word for direction. The Bible teaches us to trust in God's plan for our lives because He always knows what is best for us.

He cares for us, and He withholds nothing from us that is in our best interest. He gently guides us toward His very best for us in every situation.

When facing life's challenges, we can become emotionally weak and accept the Enemy's lies about our "missing out," feeling God is not pursuing our best interest.

Before our ancestors disobeyed God, Satan, "the Father of Lies" (John 8:44), told them they would not die from eating the forbidden fruit. Then, he inferred God withheld something priceless from them (i.e., the knowledge of good and evil).

The Lord placed them within the Garden of Eden, and He supplied them with everything they could ever want or need to have happy and fulfilled lives in a place that was free from pain, sickness, tribulation, sin, or death.

Yet, Satan's lies combined with their lusts of flesh and eyes, along with the pride of life (1 John 2:16), convinced them that God was the "villain" and that they needed more.

In the face of unsurpassed opulence and blessing, disobeying God by eating the forbidden fruit became the answer to all their questions and the solution to all their problems.

Satan's job is to confuse and distort God's perfect plan by lying and telling us that our differences make us flawed and worthless.

He has convinced many of us we are "ugly" and/or we "will not amount to anything." As a result, we live out a "self-fulfilling prophesy," convinced that our failure is inevitable.

However, God created us uniquely different by design, just as if we were pieces of a jigsaw puzzle that, when assembled, we create a beautiful portrait of His love, redemption, and glory to enhance this broken world.

Thus, we should never feel that we are mistakes or afterthoughts. God created us as male and female, with all our complexities, to fulfill His perfect, eternal design for all humanity and to bring Him honor—not the Enemy.

God has made it so that there is no other person on this earth like us. We are "fearfully and wonderfully made" in His image. (*cf.,* Genesis 1:27, Psalm 139:14)

Our bodies are extensions of His love and goodness, not the Enemy's weapons for destruction and death. We are the Lord's crowning achievements of His creation and grace to live out the plan He gave us before we were born,

> You did not choose Me, but I chose you and appointed you that you should go and bear fruit, and *that* your fruit should remain, that whatever you ask the Father in My name He may give you. (John 15:16)

We are to commit our way to Him, especially during adversity. With this biblical response, we put Him first in everything as we dedicate or rededicate our lives to Him through surrender and obedience,

> Commit your way to the Lord, Trust also in Him, And He shall bring it to pass. He shall bring forth your righteousness as the light, And your justice as the noonday. (Psalm 37:5-6)

This can be most difficult, especially when we cannot discern God's perfect will while we are in distress. It then becomes a matter of knowing what we believe and in whom we believe. (2 Timothy 1:12)

Such was the case with the Old Testament Job, who, while enduring trials, he committed his way to the Lord and gave Him glory throughout his unfortunate circumstance,

> For I know that my Redeemer lives, And He shall stand at last on the earth; And after my skin is destroyed, this I know, That in my flesh I shall see God, Whom I shall see for myself, And my eyes shall behold, and not another. How my heart yearns within me! (Job 19:25-27)

Believing that the Lord can use us—despite our circumstances—to accomplish a specific mission and purpose for us and the world is the proper biblical response to trial.

In this chapter, we explored how patience worketh experience. In the next chapter, we will look at how experience worketh hope that maketh not ashamed.

Notes

[1] See: Spiros Zodhiates, "δοκιμή," *The Complete Word Study Dictionary, New Testament*, rev. ed., (Chattanooga: AMG International, 1993) 475 and W.E. Vine, "Experience (without), Experiment," *An Expository Dictionary of New Testament Words* in *Vine's Expository Dictionary of Biblical Words*, rev. ed. (Nashville: Thomas Nelson, 1985) 218.

[2] J.P. Lange, "Epistle of Paul to the Romans," *Commentary on the Holy Scriptures: Critical, Doctrinal and Homiletical*, Philip Schaff, trans., 7th ed., vol. 10, (Grand Rapids: Zondervan, 1980) 168.

[3] James Madison Pendleton, "Personality and Deity of the Holy Spirit," *Christian Doctrines*, 33rd printing, (Valley Forge: Judson Press, 1976) 96.

[4] Charles Hodge, "The Holy Spirit," *Systematic Theology*, vol. I, 3rd printing, (Peabody: Hendrickson Publishers, 2003) 525.

[5] See: James Madison Pendleton, "Sanctification," 299

[6] Richard M. Gula, "Forming Character," *Ethics in Pastoral Ministry*, (New York: Paulist Press, 1996) 35-36.

[7] A Merriam-Webster, "Love," *Webster's New Collegiate Dictionary*, Henry Bosley Woolf, ed., (Springfield, MA: G. & C. Merriam Company, 1977) 681.

[8] For a further discussion, see: W.E. Vine, "Love (Noun and Verb)," 381- 382 and Spiros Zodhiates, "ἀγάπη," 66-67.

[9] Max Lucado, "When Crickets Make You Cranky," *When God Whispers Your Name*, (Dallas: Word Publishing, 1994) 94-95.

[10]Patrick M. Morley, "The Most Important Thing," *The Rest of Your Life*, 1st ed., (Grand Rapids: Zondervan, 1998) 179.

[11]James Madison Pendleton, "The Moral Attributes of God," *Christian Doctrines: A Compendium of Theology*, 33rd printing, (Valley Forge: Judson Press, 1976) 58.

[12]Augustus H. Strong, "Veracity and Faithfulness or Transitive Truth," *Systematic Theology*, 31st ed., (Valley Forge: Judson Press, 1976) 289.

[13]Your supervisor or HR Department can offer guidelines for reading non-work related materials during normal work hours.

Chapter Six

Chapter Six
Experience Worketh Hope that Maketh not Ashamed

God is in Control

Experience produces hope. The Greek word for hope is *"elpis,"* (Strong NT1680),[1] which describes our joyful and confident expectation to receive something wonderful with great anticipation.

From the beginning, God has had a perfect plan (or will) for His creation. He said, "Let there be!" and the heavens and earth; water and air; plants and animals appeared—instantly!

Then He said, "Let us make!" and He combined clay with His eternal Spirit; breathing into His creation the "breath of life," and thus the human species exists, and He said it was "very good!"

God designed His perfect plan for our welfare and benefit before He created the world, and He has not changed or rescinded it. God is sovereign, and everything that happens will bring about the fulfillment of that plan.

The fallen angels, Satan, our disobedience and subsequent Fall resulting in the interjection of sin and death, human free will and personal choice, wars, famine, and cataclysmic disasters can distract us from clearly seeing His glorious end, seemingly hijacking His beneficent will.

Yet, these factors do not escape His foreknowledge. The Lord will accomplish His perfect plan nonetheless, as one author observes,

> The benefit of an emphasis on God's decrees is that it helps us to realize that God does not make up plans suddenly as he goes along. He knows the end from the beginning, and will accomplish all his good purposes. This should greatly increase our trust in him, especially in difficult circumstances.[2]

Despite our failings, which are many, His unfailing plan will sustain us always,

> The steps of a good man are ordered by the Lord, And He delights in his way. Though he fall, he shall not be utterly cast down; For the Lord upholds him with His hand. I have been young, and now am old; Yet I have not seen the righteous forsaken, Nor his descendants begging bread. He is ever merciful, and lends; And his descendants are blessed. Depart from evil, and do good; And dwell forevermore. For the Lord loves justice, And does not forsake His saints; They are preserved forever, But the descendants of the wicked shall be cut off. (Psalm 37:23-28)

I rejoice knowing there is a Beneficent Creator and Infinite Sustainer who is concerned about our personal welfare and is active in our daily lives. I do not rely on the capriciousness and unreliability of happenstance, fate, chance, or luck to govern the course of our human lives.

God's unfailing design offers us the positive hope of a blessed future for this life,

> For I know the thoughts that I think toward you, says the Lord, thoughts of peace and not of evil, to give you a future and a hope. Then you will call upon Me and go and pray to Me, and I will listen to you. And you will seek Me and find Me, when you search for Me with all your heart. (Jeremiah 29: 11-13)

Yet, God has also planned a blessed hope for our eternal future with Him,

> Let not your heart be troubled; you believe in God, believe also in Me. In My Father's house are many mansions; if it were not so, I would have told you. I go to prepare a place for you. And if I go and prepare a place for you, I will come again and receive you to Myself; that where I am, there you may be also. (John 14:1-3)

The Spirit of Christ within us gives hope for eternal life. This hope is our confident and joyful expectation of future blessing based on the certainty of our salvation through Christ and of the wonderful eternal future He is preparing for us.

Flesh and blood will not inherit the Kingdom of God. (1 Corinthians 15:50) When our Lord calls us from labor to reward, we will experience the pinnacle of His redemptive plan where the wicked cease from troubling and the weary are at rest. (Job 3:17) Of this glorious transformation, the Scriptures attest,

> So when this corruptible shall have put on incorruption, and this mortal shall have put on immortality, then shall be brought to pass the saying that is written, death is swallowed up in victory. (1 Corinthians 15:54)

This is our present hope and eternal destiny or glorification. Then, God will give us immortal bodies that will resemble Christ's resurrected body. Then we can experience God's magnificent presence, free from sin, pain, and disease. We will see Him "as He is" and be like Him. (1 John 3:2)

Proud, self-righteous human endeavors will never invoke God's favor, as does Calvary's Cross. It has never been about us; it is about Jesus Christ, and our faith in Him vitalizes our being, position, conduct, and eternal destiny.

Those who will not acknowledge Him now will face Him as Eternal Judge then. However, we who love Him, and whose faith begins and ends with Him, He is our hope, peace, expectation, and glorious reward. Galatians 3:11 reads, "The just shall live by faith," and 2 Corinthians 5:7 states, "We walk by faith, not by sight."

I opened this book with my Divine Appointment. Before closing, I will share my testimony.

My Testimony
I cannot remember the exact day and time when I accepted Jesus Christ as my personal Lord and Savior. I know it was long before I was baptized at around 10 years old.

God blessed me with Christian parents. I was part of a Christian home where Mom, Dad, Grandma knew the Lord themselves, and they "feared" the Lord, and they loved Him and my brothers and I to the extent that they shared Him with us, while living a consistent Christian life simultaneously.

They were not perfect—no one is. Yet, they were consistent by taking us to church, praying, reading the Bible, and living godly lives in front of us daily. We learned how to love, since they loved us, and we learned self-respect and how to be responsible citizens in our ever-changing world.

It was the 1960s and our home had its share of issues and problems associated with our race and poverty. Still, we knew God was at its center, and He preserved and prospered us during that turbulent period.

After I came to Christ, my parents nurtured and encouraged me in my faith so that I, too, would live for Him. They were there for me when I felt led to leave home and go to Bible College and later seminary.

I hungered for a spiritual change in my life. I wanted to know more about God and His plans for me. I desired to serve the Lord and His church in a greater capacity, but I did not know where He wanted me to serve or what He wanted me to do. My desire was like the one the Psalmist expresses,

> One thing I have desired of the Lord, That will I seek: That I may dwell in the house of the Lord All the days of my life, To behold the beauty of the Lord, And to inquire in His temple. Psalm 27:4

I forsook my presuppositions and personal agendas and asked the Lord for His direction. Over time, He revealed Himself to me in a most astounding and unforgettable fashion.

Going to Bible College meant moving away from all that I had been accustomed to and was a difficult transition for me initially. Although heartbroken and weeping, my first day away from home, my parents' prayers, support, and encouragement helped to sustain me during that rough period of adjustment.

Subsequently, they supported and encouraged me when I surrendered to God's Call on my life to become a minister, and they were there to congratulate and wish me well when I married and started a family.

As the years progressed, they taught me how we can live life well and thus honor Christ—even through illness and death.

Many so-called "Christian" fads have come and gone over the years, as have people who have professed to be Christians. Some have wondered why I continue to follow Christ. My answer is quite simple.

First, it does not take a rocket scientist to see that our world is facing a pervasive "sin problem." To the casual observer, it is as if the demographic for finding heinous and diabolical ways to afflict harm indiscriminately is growing younger by the minute.

In addition, people whom you would never expect are committing atrocious acts against both family members and neighbors.

I, too, was born with a "sin problem" that distracts me from being noble consistently. Even when I want to do right, yet, I get angry and think unpleasant thoughts, or speak harshly, and act inappropriately.

Someone once described their spiritual condition before meeting Christ as being *"tore [sic] up from the floor up!"* I could identify with those sentiments concerning my sinful plight and the need for a Savior,

> O wretched man that I am! Who will deliver me from this body of death? (Romans 7:24)

Under sin's conviction, the irrationality and futility of my continuing in pride and unbelief became even clearer. For with everything I had or could ever gain on this earth, still I would not measure up to the perfection we can find in Jesus Christ.

I was under just condemnation to eternal ruin without defense or excuse. Suddenly, it occurred to me I needed a Savior and Mediator, because I could not save myself.

Second, Jesus Christ was an actual historical person, who by most accounts, is considered the most influential person in human history. On any list of the world's greatest men, we find at its head Jesus of Nazareth.

> Regardless of whether or not men acknowledge him as Savior and Lord they must pay tribute to Him as the world's outstanding man.[3]

Old Testament prophesies foretold of His miraculous birth, life, ministry and teachings, death, and resurrection with incredible detail and exactness. The New Testament features a historically factual, reliable account of these occurrences.

As God in human flesh, He was unlike any other person who has ever lived, past, present, or future, which renders the Christian faith both unique and authoritative. Jesus Christ lived and died, proclaimed and proved to be the only Son of God.[4]

His flawless yet simple teachings define and describe a New Testament Age, where we can have our sins forgiven, and have a complete spiritual transformation by faith (as opposed to our works).

In Him, we are free from the stigma and bondage of sin and death, restored to intimacy with God forever, just as He promises,

> Therefore if the Son makes you free, you shall be free indeed. (John 8:36)

The Lord is my Advocate before a holy and righteous God. He alone is my Divine Intercessor whose complete works enable Him to secure my redemption forever, as this author observes,

> He is our advocate. He appears at the bar of God for us. He pleads our cause. He presents his work of obedience and

suffering as the ground of our justification. He exerts his influence, the influence of his character as the Son of God in whom the Father is ever well pleased, and whom He heareth always, as well as the influence due to Him in virtue of the covenant of redemption, and the perfect fulfillment of its condition, and to secure for his people all the good they need.[5]

When we encounter Him personally, our disposition becomes like that of the Woman at the Well, who, after meeting Jesus, responded to other people emphatically,

> Come, see a Man who told me all things that I ever did. Could this be the Christ? (John 4:29)

There is none like Him—*anywhere!*

Finally, the Roman government, the most powerful government of the time, executed Jesus of Nazareth and guarded His tomb with armed soldiers. Although we have accounts of His death and burial, no one can account for His body, as this author explains,

> The empty tomb is that silent testimony to the resurrection of Christ, which has never been refuted. The Romans and Jews could not produce Christ's body or explain where it went, but nonetheless, they

refused to believe. Not because of the insufficiency of evidence but in spite of its sufficiency do men still reject the resurrection.[6]

No other person in human history ever predicted their death with a promise to rise from the dead, and then accomplish it, as did our Lord. His resurrection was not coming back from the dead like those He healed.

Otherwise, He would have died from old age, eventually. Instead, He has become the "first fruits" of all of us who trust in Him for our salvation. (1 Corinthians 15:20-23)

Final Thoughts
If my life-long assessment is wrong, and Jesus Christ is not who He says He was then or is now, I have endured the persecution, humiliation, and ridicule for not pursuing the educational, vocational, and socio-political pursuits of my peers, believing that such pursuits would have either distracted me from or conflicted with my service to Christ.

As a youth, I remember parting ways with people who wanted to drink and do drugs, and I did not, when it was the culture and climate at the time. For expressing how the Bible teaches that gaining wealth should not consume us as Christians, and that we should not rely on our own wisdom apart from God's wisdom (Proverbs 23:4), back in the day, I lost a very close confidant.

I was rebuffed for expressing how I wanted God to do "whatever He has to do" in me to make me whatever He wants me to be, chided about being "so heavenly minded that I am no earthly good," and told "oh, that's spiritual" after sharing how Christian's behavior should differ from the world.

I could have followed many of my contemporaries by living a modest, unassuming life without surrendering to Christ. Then I would have had to face death, with all of life being meaningless as the vanity of vanities; all is vanity! (Ecclesiastes 1:2)

Nevertheless, if my assessment is correct, and Jesus Christ is the same yesterday, today, and forever (Hebrews 13:8), *I have everything to gain!*

I have a Dear Friend, who has never left or forsaken me. In those dark moments when I have had to walk by myself, I was never alone.

Throughout my good and bad experiences and circumstances, as well as in my joys and sorrows, He has been with me. He has dried my tears, comforted me in distress, and fought my battles. His loving presence fills my heart with joy and peace. He supplies me with all the spiritual gifts, strength, and resources I need to live for Him well,

> Now to Him who is able to do exceedingly abundantly above all that we ask or think, according to the power that works in us, to Him be glory in the church

by Christ Jesus to all generations, forever and ever. Amen. (Ephesians 3:20-21)

He has blessed me immeasurably and has given me opportunities to go places, do things, and meet people I could have only imagined as a youth. He continues to answer my prayers and supply my every need. He gives me the faith I need to trust Him implicitly and follow Him daily.

These Bible passages, I cherish and hold dear,

> I had fainted, unless I had believed to see the goodness of the LORD in the land of the living. Wait on the LORD: be of good courage, and he shall strengthen thine heart: wait, I say, on the LORD. Psalm 27:13-14 (AKJV)

> For the vision *is* yet for an appointed time; But at the end it will speak, and it will not lie. Though it tarries, wait for it; Because it will surely come, It will not tarry. ... But the just shall live by his faith. (Habakkuk 2:3-4)

> He did not waver at the promise of God through unbelief, but was strengthened in faith, giving glory to God, and being fully convinced that what He had promised He was also able to perform. (Romans 4:20-21)

I believe God can and will fulfill, in full measure, every promise He has made to us. It now becomes our responsibility to trust that He will do it in the proper time and in the proper way—that suits Him!

I thank God that He continues to work within me to help foster and strengthen miraculous spiritual changes in my heart and life, and in the hearts and lives of others, in ways that yet baffle me.

I want to finish this race well as the Scriptures remind me,

> Those who sow in tears Shall reap in joy. He who continually goes forth weeping, Bearing seed for sowing, Shall doubtless come again with rejoicing, Bringing his sheaves with him. (Psalm 136:5-6)
>
> And let us not grow weary while doing good, for in due season we shall reap if we do not lose heart. (Galatians 6:9)
>
> Then I heard a voice from heaven saying to me, "Write: 'Blessed are the dead who die in the Lord from now on.' " "Yes," says the Spirit, "that they may rest from their labors, and their works follow them." (Revelation 14:13)

Mine has been a tremendous life, for there has never been a time when I did not feel His complete peace, satisfaction, and fulfillment.

Even in moments of sadness, He fills my heart with unspeakable joy, just as His word declares,

> For His anger is but for a moment, His favor is for life; Weeping may endure for a night, But joy comes in the morning. (Psalm 30:5)

He leads me down His perfect path. Daily, He affirms His Word while bringing to mind those comforting songs that tell of His goodness and faithfulness to refresh my heart.

He has blessed me with a wonderful wife and family, and He has given us some incredible relationships with people past and present who have befriended us.

Those who have gone to be with the Lord, I look forward to seeing them again along with the Saints in Heaven. For at some point, I, too, will have to finish this race well and join them with the Lord forever.

Mine is an enduring hope that maketh not ashamed, because beyond the abundant life on earth, a glorious eternal life yet awaits me. Then, I shall hear the Lord's welcoming voice affirm, *"Well done!"*

Amen and Hallelujah! What a Wonderful Savior!

Notes

[1] For a full discussion, see: Spiros Zodhiates, "ἐλπίς," *The Complete Word Study Dictionary, New Testament*, rev. ed., (Chattanooga: AMG International, 1993) 570-572, and W.E. Vine, "Hope (Noun and Verb), Hope (for)," *An Expository Dictionary of New Testament Words*, in *Vine's Expository Dictionary of Biblical Words*, rev. ed. (Nashville: Thomas Nelson, 1985) 311, and Walter Bauer, "ἐλπίς," *A Greek-English Lexicon of the New Testament and Other Early Christian Literature*, F. Wilbur Gingrich and Frederick W. Danker, ed., 2nd rev. ed., (Chicago: University of Chicago Press, 1979) 252-253, and Strong, "ἐλπίς," "Dictionary of Greek Words," *Strong's Exhaustive Concordance of the Bible*, (Iowa Falls: Riverside Book and Bible House, 19--?) 27.

[2] Wayne A. Grudem, "The Decrees of God," *Systematic Theology: An Introduction to Biblical Doctrine*, (Grand Rapids: Zondervan, 1994) 333.

[3] H.I. Hester, "The Greatness of Jesus," *The Heart of the New Testament*, 35th ed., (Nashville: Broadman Press, 1981) 5.

[4] See: Norman L. Gisler, "The Deity and Authority of Jesus Christ," *Christian Apologetics*, 5th printing, (Grand Rapids: Baker Book House, 1991) 329-352.

[5] Charles Hodge, "Christ our Intercessor," *Systematic Theology*, vol. II, 3rd printing, (Peabody: Hendrickson Publishers, 2003) 593.

[6] Josh McDowell, "The Resurrection – Hoax or History," *Evidence that Demands a Verdict: Historical Evidences for the Christian Faith*, rev. ed., vol. I, (San Bernardino: Here's Life Publishers, Inc., 1979) 226.

About the Author

Floyd Bland has been a ministry leader, teacher, chaplain, and pastor. Through Not Of The World Ministries, Inc., he offers sound, practical, Bible-based interactive models for Christian living.

Floyd has written other books including, *The Christian Heritage: God's Answers for a Searching World, Radical Forgiveness Through the Eyes of Jesus, Five Things Every Christian Must Know, Oh For The Joy! Forgiven and Free in Christ,* and *The Last Words of Jesus to His Disciples: Enduring Lessons of Faith, Hope, and Love.*

Floyd is married to his best friend and helpmate, and together they have two grown children and a grandson.

www.ingramcontent.com/pod-product-compliance
Lightning Source LLC
Chambersburg PA
CBHW071247070526
44583CB00017B/2370